Reclaiming Freedom

Life After Lock up

Michael A. Davis

Reclaiming Freedom

Copyright © 2024 by Michael A. Davis
All rights reserved.

Printed in The United States of America

No portion of this publication may be reproduced, stored in any form without written permission from the publisher or author, except for the inclusion of limited quotations in a review as permitted by U.S. copyright law.

ISBN: 9798325301926
Library of Congress Control Number: *2024910399*

First Edition: June, 2024

Michael A Davis
Austin, Texas 78702

Contents

Introduction — vii

1. REALITY OF MASS INCARCERATION — 1
   Exploring the disproportionate effects on marginalized communities, particularly people of color — 3
   The need for criminal justice reform and reentry support — 6

2. THE POWER OF SECOND CHANCES — 9
   Sharing inspiring stories of individuals who have successfully reintegrated into society after prison — 9
   Transformative potential of second chances and the importance of belief in one's capacity for change — 12
   Strategies and mindset shifts for embracing second chances and creating positive change — 17

3. UNDERSTANDING THE REENTRY
   PROCESS   20
   *The various stages of the reentry process,
   including release planning, housing,
   employment, and social support*   20
   *Practical advice for navigating these
   challenges effectively*   29
   *Discussing the role of family, friends,
   mentors, and community organizations in
   providing assistance and guidance*   31

4. EMPLOYMENT AND EDUCATION
   OPPORTUNITIES   35
   *Examining the importance of employment
   and education in successful reentry*   35
   *The barriers faced by formerly incarcerated
   individuals when seeking employment or
   pursuing education*   37
   *Resources, strategies, and ways to help
   overcome these obstacles*   39

5. OVERCOMING STIGMA AND
   REBUILDING IDENTITY   44
   *Addressing the social stigma attached to
   having a criminal history and its effect on
   self-esteem and identity*   44
   *The importance of personal narratives and
   challenging societal stereotypes*   66

6. MENTAL HEALTH AND WELL-BEING 69
   Examining the prevalence of mental health concerns among individuals transitioning back into society from imprisonment 69
   Highlight the importance of self-care, resilience and seeking support 73

7. ADVOCATING FOR CRIMINAL JUSTICE REFORM 79
   Disseminate information regarding systemic changes needed to assist successful reentry and reduce recidivism 79

   Final Words 101
   Sources 105
   Notes 115
   Notes 117

Introduction

Reentering society after incarceration can be a hard and overwhelming journey that individuals face when leaving prison. Reintegrating back into society may involve social stigmatization, limited opportunities and systemic obstacles which hinder rehabilitation efforts while making life much harder to rebuild a sense of belonging and stability for reentrants. Emphasize the importance of addressing these challenges to facilitate successful reintegration and reduce rates of recidivism.

As someone who was previously incarcerated, I understand first-hand the immense obstacles involved with reintegrating back into society after prison. Struggles between social stigma, limited opportunities, and systemic obstacles often feel insurmountable - forcing individuals into crime cycles once more. With this book I want to highlight this necessity of addressing such challenges head-on; doing so

Introduction

allows us to build societies which truly believe in second chances while offering individuals support needed to rebuild their lives successfully.

An integral element of successful reintegration after imprisonment lies in addressing social stigmas, limited opportunities and systemic barriers imposed upon individuals reentering society after imprisonment. By creating an inclusive society which offers support, opportunities and second chances, we can empower formerly incarcerated individuals to rebuild their lives, contribute positively to their communities and break free of incarceration cycles - through collective effort we can foster more just and compassionate societies that recognize everyone's inherent worth as individuals who possess untapped growth potential regardless of past mistakes.

Communities, policymakers, employers and individuals all must come together and collaborate in order to realize these goals. Policy reforms that promote fair treatment and equal opportunities for former inmates include ban-the-box measures which remove checks on job applications regarding criminal history as well as expungement/record-sealing laws which allow individuals to move beyond past convictions without restrictions imposed upon their lives by conviction records.

Support networks and mentorship programs can play an integral part in aiding successful reintegration. Mentors with similar experiences can offer guidance, encouragement, and practical advice as they navigate the complexi-

Introduction

ties of rejoining society. Community-based organizations, faith-based groups, grassroots initiatives all help form networks of support to assist with overcoming obstacles and finding an identity for all individuals involved in society reentry.

Education and awareness can play a pivotal role in breaking down barriers to inclusion. By offering educational programs at schools and community centers that foster understanding and deconstruct stereotypes, we can foster an environment which is more welcoming. Furthermore, offering workshops or training sessions specifically targeting employers or landlords may dispel misconceptions while simultaneously emphasizing opportunities available to reentry individuals.

Fostering successful reintegration and decreasing recidivism rates requires taking an integrative approach. We must address poverty, lack of access to resources, systemic inequalities and systemic injustice as the root causes for criminal behavior. By investing in rehabilitation programs, mental health services, addiction treatments and job training we can give individuals tools they need to break free from incarceration's cycle.

Through telling the stories of individuals newly released from prison and discussing the obstacles they are up against, this book seeks to inspire change and foster an environment in which redemption, forgiveness and second chances are prioritized. Only when confronting these challenges head-on can we foster an equitable society

Introduction

where those returning home have opportunities to rehabilitate themselves as contributing members of their communities as agents for positive transformation - together we can make an impactful impactful difference and secure a brighter future for us all!

You are about to embark on a new chapter of life that will allow you to shape your own destiny. You may have spent time in prison, but now you can break out and find freedom again. My own experience of incarceration has helped me to understand your fears and struggles. I know how difficult it can be. But I'm also living proof that these obstacles can be overcome for better prospects. We can all rediscover our independence and discover hidden possibilities by embarking on this journey together.

Accepting and embracing your journey is the best thing you can do, friend. No one else will be able to walk in your footsteps and that makes you stronger than anything. As you enter this new phase, forgive yourself and those who have wronged your. This will help you move on with confidence and clear goals.

You have a lot of strength and resilience within yourself. You can draw strength from the past struggles you have overcome, as these helped to shape who you are now.

Create a Vision

Think about your future with purpose and clarity, fellow travelers. Set meaningful goals and dream big. What would you like accomplish? Which passions are waiting

Introduction

for you to awaken them in you? Use your dreams as a compass to help you push past the limits that once limited you.

Find Community and Help

Don't embark on this liberation journey alone. You can find support from people who believe in and understand you. Mentors, organizations and those who have gone through similar experiences before are all able to provide you with comforting advice and remind you of your resilience when faced by doubts and feelings of self-doubt. You can maintain your self-confidence even when things are difficult by surrounding yourself with people who lift you up.

Steps to Accountability and Responsibility

I believe that the secret to personal growth is taking accountability for your actions and decisions. Accept any mistakes as an opportunity to improve; take responsibility; and commit to positive life changes. Each day is a new chance to match your goals with your actions.

Living in the present is important. While aspirations and dreams can inspire, don't forget to live and enjoy each moment. You are in the present, and your future is ahead. So cherish each step you make towards freedom every day.

I have unwavering confidence in you and your potential to succeed. I support you and strongly believe in it. It will take courage and persistence to regain your freedom following a prison sentence. However, you should make

Introduction

every effort to turn what has happened into something positive.

As you strive to create a meaningful and fulfilling life, be true to yourself. You can enjoy every moment of your journey to a prosperous future by seeking support, accepting responsibility and enjoying each step. Each step that you take is a continuation of your journey. Reclaiming freedom within reach and more than capable, embrace this freedom my friend. Seize every opportunity that comes your way!

Chapter 1

Reality of Mass Incarceration

As someone who has personally experienced mass incarceration in America, its history and impact are topics near and dear to my heart. Mass incarceration's legacy of injustice extends far beyond individuals to families, communities, and society at large. Mass incarceration dates back to the 80s during a period marked by political motivations and public fear-based enforcement policies that led to arresting more individuals, prosecuting them in court proceedings, sentencing them for lengthy prison terms as a result of three strikes laws, mandatory minimum sentencing laws and even banning parole eligibility further contributed to mass incarceration rates rising dramatically.

Mass incarceration has had devastating repercussions, particularly among marginalized communities such as African Americans and Hispanics who bear its brunt. Discriminatory practices of law enforcement officers such as racial profiling, profiling for sentencing disparity disparities have had an outsized effect, furthering poverty cycles of limited opportunities and social exclusion in these groups of society.

While incarcerated, individuals face numerous barriers that prevent rehabilitation and reintegration into society. Overcrowded prisons, inadequate healthcare, limited educational and vocational opportunities and an absence of support systems often leads to high recidivism rates as individuals attempt to rebuild their lives while living behind bars.

Mass incarceration's effects extend far beyond individuals incarcerated behind bars - families and communities are also profoundly impacted. Children whose parents are imprisoned face emotional trauma, economic instability and increased risks of entering criminal justice systems themselves; generations-long cycles of imprisonment shatter social fabric of communities leading to broken trust relationships between generations as they lose economic opportunity for generations that were previously cohered together and created economic security through cooperation among generations.

Recognizing these devastating results, there has been an ever-increasing movement to reform criminal justice over recent years. Advocates are pushing back on harsh sentencing practices; proposing restorative justice programs; increasing support for rehabilitation services and reentry assistance services. Meanwhile efforts addressing systemic inequalities as well as providing alternatives to imprisonment have gained popularity as people come to recognize the necessity for an inclusive criminal justice system that prioritizes compassion over incarceration.

At its heart, mass incarceration in America is deeply rooted in systemic injustices that have devastating repercussions for individuals, families, and communities alike. Therefore it is crucial that we continue to pursue meaningful reform, so as to ensure our criminal justice system focuses on rehabilitation, fairness, addressing any underlying causes contributing to crime as well as second chances and improving lives overall - including for those incarcerated - with regard to all its citizens including former inmates.

Exploring the disproportionate effects on marginalized communities, particularly people of color

Mass incarceration's devastating impacts on marginalized communities - specifically people of color - has been something I witnessed first-hand during my time behind bars. Biases and discriminatory practices implemented by the system have created an endless cycle of injustice which only serves to entrench existing inequalities further.

People of color face greater risks from arrest to sentencing from law enforcement, receiving harsher treatment from criminal justice systems, due to factors like profiling, implicit biases and prejudiced perceptions that lead to arrests and convictions disproportionate to rates of drug usage across racial groups. As one example of such imbalance, drug laws enforcement has often hurt communities of color despite similar levels being utilized across race groups.

After being arrested, people of color find their challenges exacerbated. Overrepresentation within prison populations demonstrates a systemic bias against them that denies equal treatment under law; limited access to quality legal representation compounds the disparate outcomes by leaving marginalized communities lacking resources necessary to mount effective defense strategies against prosecution.

Within prison environments, racial discrimination continues to color individuals' experiences of imprisonment. Equal access to educational and vocational programs widens this disparity even more and inhibits personal development and future prospects for many incarcerated individuals. Furthermore, tensions within prison environments can heighten violence further contributing to an unsafe and hostile atmosphere for inmates.

Families and communities cannot underestimate the ripple effect that higher incarceration rates among people of color has. Families become fractured as parents are removed, children growing up without positive role models are more likely to enter criminal justice systems themselves as a result. This cycle becomes intergenerational as children growing up without positive role models are likely to become embroiled in it themselves later on in their lives.

These disparities perpetuate a cycle of poverty, limited opportunities and social marginalization for many communities of color. Reentering society after being imprisoned often becomes an uphill struggle as they face barriers in finding stable housing, gainful employment and rebuilding their lives after prison release. Reminiscent of previous stigmatization from criminal records hindering essential resources while fuelling further cycles of recidivism are all hallmarks of failure for people of color reentering society after imprisonment.

Reducing the disparate impact on marginalized communities demands comprehensive criminal justice reform, from addressing systemic biases, investing in alternatives to incarceration and encouraging restorative practices to efforts such as reduced sentencing disparities, community programs and equitable access to resources and opportunities - these measures must all come together for meaningful equality within society.

Mass incarceration's detrimental impacts on marginalized communities, particularly people of color, is indicative of deep-seated inequities within our criminal justice system. Therefore, it's imperative that we act to dismantle systemic biases to ensure equal treatment and opportunity for individuals regardless of race or background - thus moving toward creating an even more just and equitable society that respects everyone's lives - including those incarcerated - alike.

The need for criminal justice reform and reentry support

At an intimate level, criminal justice reform and reentry support is something I understand first-hand as someone who was previously incarcerated. Our current system fails to properly serve individuals returning home after serving their time behind bars, yet I recognize its imperative nature and struggle as someone in recovery from jail time myself.

Criminal justice reform is necessary in order to address systemic injustices which perpetuate mass incarceration, rather than simply applying punitive measures as an easy solution. Restorative justice programs, community-based interventions and diversionary strategies offer alternatives that may break cycles of reoffending while encouraging accountability and rehabilitation.

Sentencing reform is necessary to ensuring fairness and proportionality within our criminal justice system. Mandatory minimum sentencing laws and three strike policies often result in excessively long sentences without taking account of individual circumstances, potential for growth or transformation or potential for rehabilitation. Sentencing guidelines must be revised so they prioritize rehabilitation over punishment by taking into account factors like nature of offenses committed; individual history; potential for successful reintegration into society etc.

Reentry support is critical in aiding an individual's successful return to society after time spent behind bars. Making the leap can be extremely daunting, with numerous hurdles standing between an individual and rebuilding his/her life after release from prison. Comprehensive programs which address housing, employment, healthcare services, mental health services and educational opportunities providing individuals with all of the tools and support necessary for an efficient reintegration back into society.

Education and vocational training within prisons is invaluable in equipping individuals with skills necessary for secure employment upon release, which reduces recidivism rates while simultaneously encouraging self-sufficiency and independence.

At the same time, eliminating stigma associated with criminal records is of utmost importance. Employment and housing discrimination against those with criminal histories creates an endless cycle of exclusion and marginalization that should end. Ban-the-box policies that prohibit employers from asking about criminal history on initial job applications provide individuals with equal chances to compete for available job positions.

Reform of the bail system is another crucial component of criminal justice reform. The current cash bail system disproportionately burdens individuals from marginalized communities who cannot afford the payments necessary for release from pretrial detention; this results in unnecessary pretrial detention that only worsens disparities within the system. Implementing alternatives such as risk evaluation and community supervision could ensure public safety while upholding "innocent until proven guilty".

Criminal justice reform and reentry support is needed urgently in order to address the shortcomings of our current system and create a fairer society. By prioritizing rehabilitation, sentencing reform, access to education programs, comprehensive reentry programs and comprehensive reentry support we can give individuals who have been imprisoned the tools to reintegrate successfully and reduce recidivism rates. Recognizing their humanity while giving them opportunities for rebuilding lives that contribute positively towards communities is also paramount in creating just and equitable societies.

Chapter 2

The Power of Second Chances

Sharing inspiring stories of individuals who have successfully reintegrated into society after prison

There are numerous inspiring individuals who have successfully transitioned back into society after jail or prison, showing resilience, determination and the transformative potential of second chances. Below are just a few examples:

1. Bryan Stevenson: Bryan Stevenson, an esteemed lawyer and founder of the Equal Justice Initiative, has dedicated his life to fighting for fairness and equity. Seeing first-hand the unjust treatment of prisoners under imprisonment, Stevenson became committed to reforming criminal justice systems - helping exonerate innocent individuals on

death row while also advocating for fair sentencing and rehabilitation programs.

2. Topeka K. Sam: Topeka K. Sam is an advocate for criminal justice reform and founder of Ladies of Hope Ministries. After serving three years for drug-related charges in federal prison, Sam dedicated herself to aiding other women successfully transition back into society after imprisonment - providing resources, support, advocacy services to break cycles of recidivism while aiding their recovery from prison life and rebuild their lives successfully.

3. Shaka Senghor is an author, mentor, and motivational speaker who successfully transformed his life after serving 19 years incarcerated - including seven in solitary confinement for murder - for conviction. While in jail he focused on personal growth by studying more in depth while becoming a positive force within prison walls. When released he took to speaking publicly as an advocate for criminal justice reform by sharing his story in order to generate change and foster healing among others.

4. Susan Burton: Susan Burton is an outstanding advocate for former inmates, having founded A New Way of Life Reentry Project after experiencing addiction and imprisonment herself. Through New Way of Life Reentry Project she provides housing, support services, education opportunities and employment to assist women as they rebuild their lives and reenter society after experiencing periods of incarceration.

5. Jeffrey Deskovic: Jeffrey Deskovic was wrongfully charged with rape and murder at 17 and spent 16 years behind bars before being exonerated using DNA evidence. Since being set free, Deskovic has dedicated his life to criminal justice reform advocacy as well as supporting wrongfully accused people through The Jeffrey Deskovic Foundation for Justice which works to prevent further convictions as well as assist exonerees transition back into society.

6. Darwin Hamilton, is The Director of Financial Management (Texas State Office of Risk Management) His personal mission is to change criminal justice policies and practices and reduce the stigma of formerly incarcerated people. He does this through his own example, and through his inspiring and powerful story-telling. Since 2012, he has worked as an activist, advocate and strategist on state and local criminal justice policy reform and provides technical assistance to the University of Texas, municipal agencies and delivered keynote speeches for social justice organizations. He has testified before Austin City Council and House Committees of the Texas Legislature.

These individuals, among many others, have demonstrated resilience by channeling personal struggles into driving forces for change and making significant contributions to society. Their stories illustrate redemption and rehabilitation possibilities while reminding us the necessity for creating an equitable criminal justice system which recognizes humanity and potential transformation within all individuals.

Michael A. Davis

Transformative potential of second chances and the importance of belief in one's capacity for change

Second chances can have life-altering results and I know from first-hand experience that believing in oneself and your ability for change has an incalculable positive influence on rehabilitation and reintegration efforts.

Society tends to view individuals incarcerated by society through the lens of past mistakes, creating the perception that these people cannot change and will repeat past offenses. Unfortunately, such an approach fails to acknowledge each person's individual ability for change regardless of past actions taken against them.

Believing in one's capacity for change can be an immensely powerful source of personal transformation. The first step toward change lies within; all it requires is for individuals to envision an alternate future free from their mistakes and circumstances that led them into prison in the first place. Belief provides hope, which inspires individuals on their search for growth opportunities such as education or self-improvement programs.

Accessing educational programs, vocational training and mental health support services within prison environments is often sufficient for personal growth. By learning new skills, knowledge and self-awareness techniques they gain empowerment and purpose while uncovering talents they might never have known they had existed before.

Reclaiming Freedom

Support systems who believe in an individual's capacity for change are also invaluable during the reentry process, from family, friends, mentors and community organizations providing guidance, encouragement, support networks. When placed within such environments individuals are more likely to successfully transition back into society.

Numerous success stories demonstrate the transformative potential of second chances: individuals who have overcome the hardships associated with incarceration and rebuilt their lives after release are living proof that one's past mistakes do not determine one's future. By seizing opportunities for personal development and taking advantage of second chances, people not only transformed themselves but have become agents for change within their communities as well.

People who have battled addiction can find redemption and become advocates for recovery by sharing their personal accounts to inspire others and spread knowledge of rehabilitation services and support available. Former inmates can use their firsthand knowledge of criminal justice reform efforts by drawing attention to flaws within the system while advocating for fair treatment of all.

Belief in one's ability for change can be an effective weapon against recidivism. By giving individuals an opportunity to reintegrate back into society with support, resources, and faith in their potential they may break free of incarceration cycles and contribute positively to society in new ways. Through rehabilitation efforts focused on rehabilitation issues as well as accessing education employment housing services we create environments in which individuals thrive while contributing positively.

Society must embrace a belief in second chances as a core value, providing opportunities for redemption to fostering an atmosphere of kindness, forgiveness and empathy that not only benefits those directly affected by imprisonment but also strengthens communities as a whole. When we recognize every individual's potential to change we create an atmosphere conducive to personal growth, healing, social reintegration and societal reconciliation.

Second chances and believing in one's capacity to change can be an amazing force that transforms lives and communities. By acknowledging our innate human potential for development and providing support and resources for redemption we can break the cycle of incarceration while creating an inclusive society which values rehabilitation, second chances, and positive contributions of each member of its population. Together let's foster an environment in which individuals feel empowered to transform their lives while society as a whole embraces second chances as part of our society's core value system.

As well as acknowledging the transformative potential of second chances and trusting in one's capacity for change, it is also crucial to acknowledge a compassionate and rehabilitative approach to criminal justice. When individuals receive opportunities to rebuild their lives after imprisonment, its ripples of positive transformation reach far beyond individuals themselves.

An important benefit is lowering recidivism rates. By investing in rehabilitation and providing individuals with needed support and resources, we can break the cycle of reoffending. When people possess skills, education and employment opportunities necessary for success they're less likely to return to a life of crime; not only is this beneficial to public safety but it reduces strains placed upon both criminal justice system and society as a whole.

Belief in second chances fosters an inclusive and compassionate society, sending an important signal that individuals should not solely be defined by past mistakes; their capacity for change should instead be recognized and celebrated. By rejecting stigmatization or permanent exclusion as permanent solutions, we create an environment in which more individuals seek assistance for themselves or take accountability for their actions as part of contributing meaningfully to communities around them.

Individuals who have experienced incarceration should be given every chance to reintegrate successfully back into society; doing so has far-reaching advantages that benefit not only themselves, but their families and communities as a whole. Strong family ties provide essential support, stability and overall well-being benefits when individuals reentering society - by offering avenues for family reunion and strengthening existing ties, we can promote healthier family dynamics while breaking intergenerational cycles of imprisonment.

Once individuals who had been imprisoned successfully reintegrate, they become invaluable members of society. Individuals who have endured the challenges associated with incarceration often develop unique perspectives and an in-depth knowledge of criminal justice system issues; their personal experiences allow them to advocate for reform, challenge stereotypes, promote policies that prioritize rehabilitation, fairness and equality as a result - amplifying these voices is key in creating an equitable and inclusive society where everyone benefits.

Second chances align closely with principles of social justice and human rights. They recognize that individuals deserve dignity, respect, and the chance to rebuild their lives with dignity and respect. By acknowledging and addressing inequalities that contribute to mass incarceration we move closer towards an equitable society which values everyone's wellbeing and potential equally.

Overall, accepting second chances and trusting oneself benefits not only those who have been imprisoned but society as a whole. Reducing recidivism rates, foster inclusivity among families and empowering communities as a result. We should advocate for criminal justice reform with regard to reentry support as we acknowledge everyone has potential to grow, heal and contribute positively towards building up communities around them.

Strategies and mindset shifts for embracing second chances and creating positive change

Adopting second chances and cultivating positive change requires adopting strategies and changing ones mindset in a combination of steps and mindset shifts. Through my time spent incarcerated, I have gained valuable insight into what it takes to embrace a fresh start, create lasting change within oneself and society at large and embrace second chances with open arms. Below are strategies and mindset changes which could aid this journey:

1. **Self-Reflection and Accountability:** Take some time to reflect upon your past actions and their outcomes, acknowledge any harm done, and accept responsibility for past errors. Self-reflection fosters personal development while setting the groundwork for positive transformation.

2. **Growth Mindset:** Adopt an attitude characterized by growth, learning and resilience. Recognize that your past does not determine your future and that personal transformation is possible. Have faith in your ability to change while remaining open-minded towards new skillsets, knowledge bases and perspectives.

3. **Setting Goals**: For success and fulfillment in life, set realistic and meaningful goals that encompass various areas such as education, employment, relationships and personal development. Having a vision of where you wish to go provides purpose and direction - creating the chance for personal transformation along the way!

4. **Seeking Support:** Seek support from family, friends, mentors and community organizations that believe in you as an agent of change - they'll offer guidance, encouragement and practical help along the way! Forming this kind of network will enable you to navigate reentry's many hurdles while continuing onward towards positive transformations.

5. **Education and Skill Building:** Make use of education opportunities, vocational training programs, and skill building programs both during and post incarceration to strengthen employability, broaden perspectives, open doors to new possibilities, and promote personal growth.

6. **Addressing Underlying Issues:** It is important to identify and treat any underlying issues which have led to past actions or involvement with criminal justice system, whether this means therapy, counseling or substance abuse treatment - this way you will better understand yourself as well as develop healthier coping mechanisms.

7. **Cultivate Gratitude and Practice Mindfulness:** Cultivate gratitude and practice mindfulness while you navigate your second chance at life. Appreciate all that good has come your way and value the opportunities afforded you by life's challenges, with mindfulness helping stay present, make conscious choices and build resilience to overcome hurdles along your journey.

8. **Advocacy and Giving Back:** Utilize your experiences and insights to become an agent of change within

your community - this energizes not only yourself but those around you as well. Becoming an agent of transformation gives us all a boost of empowerment!

9. **Patience and Perseverance:** Practice patience when making changes that require time, as setbacks can occur along the journey. Remain committed, push through difficulties, and celebrate smaller victories along the way!

10. **Acceptance and Redemption:** Embark upon an attitude of redemption and forgiveness. By recognising your capacity for change, accepting responsibility, learning from mistakes made along the way and positively contributing back into society; you can become an example for other to believe in second chances as well.

Accepting second chances and creating positive change requires adopting multiple strategies and mindset shifts, including self-reflection, growth mindset cultivation, goal setting, support seeking, education acquisition/acquisition skills acquisition/acquisition as well as practicing gratitude/mindfulness/mindfulness practice/mindful awareness practice advocated change advocacy redemption individuals who have been imprisoned can embark upon an incredible personal transformational journey that has the power to positively alter lives and communities alike.

Chapter 3

Understanding the Reentry Process

The various stages of the reentry process, including release planning, housing, employment, and social support

Reentry from imprisonment to society can be an intricate and challenging journey that individuals must navigate on their return home from incarceration. I know first-hand why each stage must be met with careful planning, perseverance and the aid of various resources if one hopes for successful reintegration back into society. Here is an outline of its key stages.

1. **Release Planning:** Individuals typically engage in release planning prior to release from confinement, working collaboratively with correctional staff, counselors and support organizations to devise an individualized transition plan tailored specifically for them. Release plan-

ning may involve researching housing options, developing employment strategies and connecting with social support networks - in addition to considering any legal or financial obligations or liabilities they might encounter upon leaving custody. Limited Reentry Programs and Services, Limits access to reentry services such as job training, educational programs and mental health supports can impede individuals in creating comprehensive release plans.

Legal and Administrative Delays: Delays in processing paperwork such as identification documents or outstanding legal issues can prolong the release planning process and hinder individuals in transitioning back into society.

Lack of Individualized Support: Reentry plans that do not account for each person's unique needs, strengths and challenges may fail to address underlying factors which contributed to their involvement with criminal justice system.

2. **Housing:** Securing stable housing is one of the cornerstones of successful reentry, yet finding suitable accommodations may prove challenging due to discriminatory rental markets for individuals with criminal records. Luckily, Reentry programs and community organizations can assist people in finding transitional or supportive housing options such as transitional, halfway houses or supportive options that provide individuals a safe space to rebuild their lives in society without fearing discrimination in renting markets; access to such programs with ban dis-

criminatory clauses are crucial in guaranteeing positive housing results for reentry outcomes!

Limited housing options and financial constraints can leave individuals leaving prison directly into homelessness, leaving them more susceptible to issues like substance abuse and reoffending. residential restrictions. An individual could find themselves facing residency restrictions that limit where they can live, further narrowing down housing options while potentially interrupting family or social connections. Unstable Living Situations: Unstable living arrangements such as transitional housing or moving frequently may hamper an individual's efforts to establish stability in his/her life and rebuild.

3. **Employment:** Finding meaningful work after imprisonment is vitally important to financial security and self-sufficiency, yet those with criminal records often encounter considerable barriers due to stigmatized perceptions or limited job prospects. Reentry programs may offer vocational training, job placement assistance and connections with employers willing to offer individuals second chances, exploring entrepreneurship or developing marketable skills can offer alternative paths into employment as well. It is vital for society and employers alike to recognize the value of fair chance hiring practices while tapping into talents of former incarcerated individuals for tapping their talents and potential.

Individuals without access to vocational training programs and job placement support during incarceration often do not possess the required skills, work experience and job readiness needed for secure and sustained employment. This problem can become further compounded if vocational programs and support for job seekers during imprisonment are restricted or unavailable.

Legal Barriers: Certain industries or occupations may impose legal constraints that prohibit individuals with certain criminal convictions from working within those fields, further diminishing their employment options. Employer Bias and Stigma: Discrimination by employers unwilling to hire individuals with criminal backgrounds can create significant hurdles to employment regardless of an applicant's qualifications and readiness to work.

4. **Social Support:** Establishing an effective support network during reentry is crucial. This may involve family, friends, mentors or community organizations providing emotional and practical help; supporting relationships help individuals navigate challenges related to reentry while maintaining motivation and building sense of belonging - peer support groups can offer invaluable connections while initiatives that promote inclusivity reduce stigma are vital in creating an ideal reentry environment for individuals during this process.

Social Support: means Re-establishing Family and Community Ties: Reestablishing trust within families and communities can be a complex, arduous journey that demands open dialogue, understanding, patience and forgiveness from everyone involved.

Individuals without strong support systems may struggle to access emotional, practical and financial help during their reentry process; increasing the risk of isolation and recidivism.

Peer Influence and Pressure: Reentering an environment where negative influences or peer pressure contributed to criminal involvement presents ongoing obstacles for maintaining positive social bonds and making prosocial choices.

5. **Rebuild Relationship:** Rebuilding Relationships take the initiative to renew relationships with family and friends by showing your regret, showing personal growth, and keeping communication channels open. Keep in mind that rebuilding trust may take some time; be patient as the process continues.

Build Supportive Communities: Connect with local support groups, faith-based organizations or community programs which offer safe and supportive spaces for reentry individuals. Being around people who understand your journey will bring comfort and provide encouragement along the way.

Create Healthy Boundaries: Surround yourself with positive influences and set boundaries with anyone who may impede your progression. Select relationships which support and align with your values and aspirations for growth and happiness.

6. **Health and Well-Being:** Addressing physical and mental health needs during reentry is of vital importance

to individuals returning to society after imprisonment, such as untreated medical conditions or mental health disorders that arise during imprisonment. Accessing healthcare services - physical/mental healthcare treatment/counseling programs as well as substance abuse reduction efforts - plays a critical role in supporting individuals overall wellness while decreasing risks of recidivism. Working collaboratively among healthcare providers, correctional institutions, community organizations, etc is required in ensuring continuity of care/support as individuals transition back into society after release incarceration.

Stigma and Access to Treatment: Mental and substance use issues can impose stigma that prevents individuals from seeking necessary support or receiving needed treatments and remedies.

Trauma and Post-Incarceration Syndrome: Many individuals leaving prison have experienced trauma both during and before incarceration; this may affect both their mental health and overall well-being.

Disrupted Medication Routines: Individuals living with chronic health conditions or mental health diagnoses may encounter difficulties accessing their prescribed medications on a consistent basis and maintaining continuity of care, leading to possible health complications and leading to potential harm in terms of compliance or noncompliance with treatment recommendations.

Your, physical, mental, and emotional well-being is equally important if not more so compared with what others experience during reentry services tailored specifically towards individuals in reentry services specialized specifically tailored toward individuals in reentry services.

Establish Healthcare Connections: Make connections with healthcare providers who specialize in serving individuals with criminal backgrounds. Prioritize regular check-ups, address any existing health conditions and adhere to any medication regimen or treatment plans as appropriate.

Adopt Positive Lifestyle Choices: Make deliberate steps toward adopting a healthier lifestyle by forgoing substance abuse, developing positive coping mechanisms, and seeking help should addiction or mental health challenges present themselves.

Reentry requires resilience, perseverance and an optimistic growth mindset if it's going to go smoothly. Stay focused on your goals while seeking support if necessary - each day presents itself as an opportunity! Focus on growth and progress while celebrating your achievements along the way. Through perseverance and positive thought patterns, it is possible to overcome all barriers and build a fulfilling life outside incarceration.

7. **Compliance With Legal Obligations:** Adherence to legal obligations such as parole and probation requirements can play a pivotal role in the reentry process, including regular check-ins with parole or probation offi-

cers, attending programs or counseling sessions mandated by law courts, and adhering to specific conditions set by them is integral for maintaining freedom and successfully reintegrating into society; reform efforts that promote fair sentencing as well as evidence-based practices can contribute to positive reentry outcomes.

Legal Obligations and Violation Risks: Strict Compliance With Probation/Parole Conditions can Be Challenging Even minor violations could mean being sent back into custody and this pressure can become overwhelming and stressful for individuals on parole/probation. This additional pressure adds further anxiety.

Limited Legal Assistance: People without sufficient means often encounter difficulty navigating complex legal processes alone and, consequently, may face potential challenges and have limited understanding of their rights and responsibilities.

Overcriminalization: For certain individuals, overly punitive legal systems create an endless cycle of involvement with criminal justice systems that makes successful reentry more challenging.

Financial Aid: Financial obstacles such as restrictions to federal financial aid for higher education may impede individuals in taking advantage of educational opportunities that would foster growth as individuals strive towards furthering their personal development and future plans.

Reintegration to Educational Settings: Reintegrating into traditional schools or correctional education programs may pose challenges related to social adaptation, academic gaps and feelings of inadequacy.

Negative Self-Perception: Individuals may struggle with negative self-perceptions and an unwillingness to believe they possess the capacity for personal development and success, making overcoming internal obstacles integral for taking full advantage of educational and personal development initiatives.

Recognizing and responding to these challenges will enable us to develop comprehensive reentry programs and support systems to offer individuals all of the tools, resources, and opportunities needed for them to successfully reintegrate back into society. It is vitally important that reentry be approached with empathy, understanding, fairness and dedication towards creating an atmosphere conducive to positive changes while offering second chances.

8. **Education and Personal Development:** Engaging in education and personal development opportunities during reentry can have a transformative effect. Acquiring educational credentials such as high school diploma or college degrees opens doors to better employment prospects while engaging in personal development programs, workshops or vocational training enhances skills development as well as personal growth and self-confidence development. Accessible yet affordable educational options both within correctional facilities as well as within

communities is crucial in order to promote successful reentry while decreasing chances of future involvement with criminal justice system.

Each stage of reentry poses its own set of difficulties, but with proper planning, determination, and support from various resources available to individuals they can successfully navigate them. Society needs to recognize this critical need by offering comprehensive support, access to resources, and opportunities for personal growth when individuals reentering society reintegrate successfully while decreasing recidivism rates. By investing in support services dedicated to reentry as well as policies which promote fair opportunities while eliminating barriers we can contribute towards creating an inclusive society which accepts each person no matter their past transgressions.

Practical advice for navigating these challenges effectively

When developing a release plan, seek assistance from programs, social workers or community organizations who specialize in supporting individuals during reentry processes. They may offer guidance and resources that will enable you to put together an effective release strategy plan.

Set Clear Goals for reentry establish short and long-term reentry goals such as housing acquisition, job finding, reconnecting with family and friends and more. Break these objectives down into smaller, manageable steps so as to stay focused and motivated throughout.

Build a support network surrounding yourself with people who believe in your potential for change and offer their help and encouragement throughout your journey. Look to mentors, support groups or reentry organizations to guide and encourage you on this path to change.

Research Available Resources for Individuals with Criminal Records. Explore transitional housing programs, nonprofit organizations or government initiatives which offer housing assistance for people with a criminal history. Investigate local housing laws and regulations so you understand your rights and any possible barriers or stumbling blocks you might face when renting accommodation.

Create a housing plan outline your budget, preferred locations and any specific housing requirements in order to develop an actionable Housing Plan. Work with agencies or landlords willing to accommodate individuals with criminal records.

Build a positive rental history where possible, collect references from employers, parole or probation officers, or community leaders that can vouch for your reliability and commitment to stability; this may help alleviate potential landlord concerns about renters who do not yet possess one.

Sharpen Your Skills: For better chances at employment, expand your qualifications through vocational or educational programs or skill building workshops that specialize in your desired area, such as those offering certifications or credentials that are in demand in that sector.

Create an Effective Resume: Tailor your resume to highlight your strengths, transferable skills, and any relevant work experience. Focus on showing evidence of personal development while simultaneously showing commitment and positive contributions within the workforce.

Utilize Supportive Networks: Engage organizations that assist people with criminal records in finding employment. They usually have established relationships with employers who welcome second chances for these job candidates. Networking within your own community or through personal connections could also open doors.

Discussing the role of family, friends, mentors, and community organizations in providing assistance and guidance

Mental health concerns among individuals transitioning back into society following imprisonment is an acute worry and requires special consideration and assistance. Studies and reports have shed light on their high rates of mental illness - here are a few key points backed up with sources:

1. High Prevalence of Mental Health Disorders:

According to research published in the American Journal of Public Health, people leaving prison have an elevated prevalence of mental health disorders than the general population (Binswanger et al. 2010).

2. Co-Occurrence of Substance Abuse and Mental Health Disorders:

It is unfortunately common among individuals transitioning out of prison to experience co-occurring mental health and substance use issues simultaneously.

- According to the National Institute on Drug Abuse (NIDA), substance abuse and mental health conditions often overlap, with substance use serving as a form of self-medication (NIDA, 2018).

3. Barriers to Achieve Mental Healthcare:

- Formerly Incarcerated Individuals have difficulty accessing mental healthcare services and support due to significant access barriers.

A report issued by the Council of State Government Justice Center revealed that individuals leaving prison experience difficulty accessing healthcare and community resources (CSG Justice Center 2017).

4. Imprisonment's Effect on Mental Health:

- The experience of imprisonment itself can either aggravate or contribute to mental health concerns. Research published by JAMA Psychiatry suggests that trauma, stress and stigmatization associated with imprisonment may contribute to or worsen mental health problems (Wang et al. 2018).

5. Importance of Comprehensive Reentry Programs:

It is vitally important for successful community reintegration that comprehensive reentry programs address mental health needs when looking at successful reentry.

RAND Corporation conducted a study highlighting the efficacy of comprehensive programs offering mental health services, substance abuse treatment and support to decrease recidivism while simultaneously improving mental health outcomes (Davis et al. 2013).

Addressing the mental health needs of individuals transitioning out of incarceration requires taking an integrated approach which includes greater access to mental health services, targeted interventions, and comprehensive reentry support services. By acknowledging and responding effectively to mental health challenges in this population and using evidence-based strategies for change we can work toward improved results and facilitate successful community reintegration.

As someone who has personally experienced imprisonment, I understand first-hand the crucial importance of family, friends, mentors and community organizations in providing assistance and guidance during the reentry process. Supportive family, friends and networks can make all the difference on our journey toward successful reintegration. I understand the difficulty involved with reentering society can be formidable; success requires resilience, determination and an effective support network. Let us embrace the support, guidance, and assistance offered by loved ones and the community to defy odds, change narratives, and craft futures filled with purpose, growth, and contribution. Each of us are defined not by past mistakes but by how successfully they rise above them and create lives filled with meaningful purposeful lives that create fulfillment in life.

Family, friends, mentors and community organizations create an important network of support which equips us to overcome difficulties and accept second chances in our lives. They offer us guidance that enables us to rebuild ourselves from scratch while discovering who we truly are in spite of challenges that may come our way. Through their collective efforts we find hope despite hardship.

Chapter 4

Employment and Education Opportunities

Examining the importance of employment and education in successful reentry

As both a life coach and someone who has experienced imprisonment first hand, I understand the integral role employment and education play in successful reentry after experiencing significant life transitions or setbacks. Focusing on employment and education can help restore your confidence while rebuilding life for an abundant future - we will explore their importance further below.

First and foremost, employment provides financial security and purposeful work that allows individuals to meet basic needs as well as contribute to society and live fulfilling lives. Engaging in meaningful work gives one identity, self-worth, structure to the day, and regaining control over one's life; setting goals, planning ahead for better futures etc can all become possible again once employment has been secured.

Employment promotes both personal and skill development. You have opportunities to learn new things, improve existing ones, gain valuable experience and ultimately increase employability - opening doors to higher paying and more fulfilling career options. Furthermore, workplace skills like teamwork communication problem-solving may translate well to everyday situations helping strengthen relationships while managing challenges more successfully.

Education plays a pivotal role in successful reentry. By investing in your knowledge and developing new skills through educational pursuits, education provides you with a path towards fulfilling your desired career paths - be that through degree programs, certification programs or professional development courses. By investing in yourself through this avenue you increase employability and increase chances of finding meaningful employment.

Education equips you with critical thinking skills, problem-solving abilities and a wider perspective of the world. Education builds confidence while feeding curiosity. Furthermore, it can boost self-esteem and motivation during the reentry process while acting as a springboard towards personal and professional advancement - breaking through any barriers or hurdles which have previously inhibited your progression in any capacity.

Employment and education are integral parts of successful reentry. Employment offers financial security, purposeful work life experiences, personal growth opportunities and professional skills development opportunities; while education offers knowledge, skills development and broadened perspectives. By prioritizing both aspects, you can rebuild your life, restore confidence and build an exciting new future - it may take longer but with dedication, resilience, perseverance and an eagerness for self-improvement you can unlock all your full potential and achieve lasting success!

The barriers faced by formerly incarcerated individuals when seeking employment or pursuing education

As someone who has personally endured imprisonment and experienced its challenges of reentry, I can shed light on some of the obstacles former inmates often encounter when seeking employment or education opportunities. While such obstacles may appear daunting at first, they should be addressed honestly so we can create more inclusive societies offering equal access.

One of the primary barriers is associated with having a criminal record. Employers may hesitate to hire people with past arrest records due to preconceived notions regarding reliability, trustworthiness and potential risk in the workplace; often leading to rejection and limited job opportunities resulting in difficulty in finding stable employment. Furthermore, certain jobs may even legally forbid certain convictions further narrowing employment options available to candidates.

One barrier is lack of educational opportunities. Many formerly incarcerated individuals face limited education backgrounds due to time behind bars; when trying to pursue studies they typically encounter financial restrictions and limited resources that make accessing scholarships, grants or any financial aid options near impossible - making acquiring skills for career advancement or personal advancement all that much harder.

Housing instability presents another significant barrier for individuals reentering society. Finding stable and affordable housing is always challenging; finding safe housing even harder with convictions on record as many landlords and housing providers have policies which prevent individuals with convictions from renting there - making finding safe housing even harder to secure than before! Without secure accommodation it becomes even harder to maintain employment or pursue educational programs.

Lacking support networks and resources, many individuals leaving prison face social isolation with few positive role models or mentors to turn to for advice or guidance when entering either the job market or educational institutions successfully. Without guidance and encouragement it becomes harder to navigate these environments effectively.

Formerly incarcerated individuals face many barriers when seeking employment or education after release from imprisonment, such as stigmatization, limited educational opportunity access and housing instability - just to name a few obstacles they face. Addressing these difficulties involves social changes such as reducing stigmatization by offering educational opportunities or reforming housing policies; building comprehensive reentry programs providing support; or offering inclusive and supportive environments so formerly incarcerated people can begin rebuilding their lives, contributing meaningfully back into society, while becoming valued members of communities where we all reside together.

Resources, strategies, and ways to help overcome these obstacles

- Having faced these obstacles myself, I understand the importance of resources, strategies, and ways to overcome the challenges that formerly incarcerated individuals encounter when seeking employment or pursuing education. Here are some suggestions that can help navigate the reentry process and work towards a brighter future:

1. *Expungement and Record Sealing*: Research the possibility of expunging or sealing your criminal record. This process varies by jurisdiction, but it can help reduce the

stigma associated with a criminal record and increase employment prospects.

2. *Rehabilitation Programs:* Take advantage of rehabilitation programs offered within correctional facilities or in the community. These programs provide valuable skills training, education, and counseling services to help you reintegrate successfully.

3. *Reentry Programs and Organizations:* Connect with reentry programs and organizations that offer resources and support tailored to the needs of formerly incarcerated individuals. These programs often provide job placement assistance, educational support, housing referrals, and mentorship opportunities.

4. *Job Training and Skill Development:* Seek out vocational training programs that offer specific skills needed in high-demand industries. These programs can equip you with marketable skills and increase your chances of securing employment.

5. *Networking and Mentorship:* Build a support network of individuals who have successfully navigated the reentry process or are supportive of second chances. Seek mentorship opportunities that can provide guidance, advice, and connections to potential employers or educational institutions.

6. *Continuing Education:* Explore educational opportunities such as community college programs, trade schools, or online courses. Many institutions offer support services

for individuals with criminal backgrounds, including financial aid options and academic counseling.

7. *Personal Development:* Invest in personal growth by participating in workshops, seminars, and self-improvement programs. These activities can enhance your self-esteem, communication skills, and emotional well-being, making you more competitive in the job market.

8. *Local Support Services:* Research local resources and support services available to formerly incarcerated individuals. These may include transitional housing programs, employment assistance centers, legal aid clinics, and counseling services.

9. *Advocate for Policy Change:* Join advocacy groups that work to reform policies and eliminate barriers faced by formerly incarcerated individuals. By sharing your experiences and advocating for change, you can help create a more inclusive society.

10. *Persistence and Resilience:* Finally, maintain a positive mindset and stay resilient in the face of obstacles. Reentry can be challenging, but with perseverance and determination, you can overcome the barriers and achieve your goals.

Remember, you are not alone in this journey. Reentering society after incarceration can feel overwhelming, but there are people and organizations ready to support you every step of the way. Reach out for support from family, friends, or mentors who believe in your potential and want to see you succeed. They can provide emotional encouragement, offer guidance, and help you stay motivated during challenging times.

In addition to your personal network, make use of the available resources designed specifically for individuals in reentry. Explore organizations that focus on assisting formerly incarcerated individuals with employment, education, housing, and other critical needs. These resources may include reentry programs, non-profit organizations, or government agencies that offer specialized services tailored to your circumstances.

When it comes to employment, seek out programs that provide job readiness training, resume building, and interview preparation. These programs can help you highlight your skills and experience while addressing any concerns employers may have about your criminal record. Some organizations even offer job placement services or partnerships with companies that are open to hiring individuals with criminal backgrounds.

For education, research educational institutions that have programs or initiatives supporting the educational goals of individuals with criminal records. Look for scholarships, grants, or tuition assistance programs specifically designed for individuals in reentry. Community colleges often offer flexible schedules and a supportive environment, making them a great option for pursuing further education or skill development.

Beyond external resources, focus on your personal growth and mindset. Cultivate a positive attitude and believe in your ability to overcome obstacles. Embrace opportunities for self-reflection, self-improvement, and personal development. Consider joining support groups or participating in counseling or therapy to address any emotional or psychological challenges that may arise during the reentry process.

It's important to recognize that building a fulfilling and successful life after incarceration takes time and effort. Be patient with yourself and celebrate every small achievement along the way. Set realistic goals and develop a plan to achieve them. Remember, setbacks are a natural part of the journey, but with determination and perseverance, you can overcome them and continue moving forward.

Believe in your potential and the positive changes you can make in your life. Surround yourself with individuals who uplift and support you. Stay focused on your personal growth, education, and employment goals. With the right mindset, support network, and a commitment to your own success, you can navigate the challenges of reentry and build a life full of purpose, fulfillment, and achievement.

Chapter 5

Overcoming Stigma and Rebuilding Identity

Addressing the social stigma attached to having a criminal history and its effect on self-esteem and identity

Today I would like to address an issue which threatens our self-esteem and identity: social stigma associated with criminal records. Having gone through myself the challenges associated with reintegrating into society after imprisonment, I can sympathize with your burden but am here as your guide in helping regain your self-worth with strength and resilience.

Stigma's Impact on Personal Identity:

A criminal history often invites judgment and prejudice from society. Stigma often infiltrates our psyche, leaving us feeling isolated, ashamed, and powerless over our narrative - yet, by accepting responsibility and moving on we have the ability to rewrite history for future success!

Rebuilding Self Esteem: 1. Acceptance and Forgiveness: The first step to rebuilding self-esteem lies in accepting your past mistakes as responsibility and showing kindness toward both yourself and others as part of healing and moving forward with life. Embark upon forgiveness both towards oneself as well as others.

2. Self-Reflection and Personal Growth: Use your experiences as opportunities to reflect upon yourself. Identify areas for improvement and set realistic goals, whether through education, therapy or simply developing new skills. Recognize and believe in yourself - recognize potential strengths within yourself that you could change!

3. Positive Self-Talk: Replace negative self-talk with affirming statements to increase positivity within yourself and surround yourself with supportive people who uphold and inspire. Celebrate all accomplishments no matter how small and remind yourself of your inherent worthiness. Celebrate successes no matter their scale while reminding yourself to celebrate life!

Rediscover Your Identity:

1. *Celebrate Your Unique Journey:* Your past does not define who you are entirely; embrace its significance for shaping you into who you are now, sharing it when the time is right in order to promote understanding and break stereotypes.

2. *Define Your Values and Passions:* Rebuilding your identity involves rediscovering what truly matters to you. Reflect on your values, interests, passions and activities which bring pleasure or fulfillment and find fulfillment from these activities. By staying true to yourself you can reshape your identity according to what reflects who you truly are - this way rebuilding can begin at its source!

3. *Contributing and Giving Back:* Finding purpose through giving is an effective way of rebuilding identity. Look for opportunities to give back to the community, share skills or offer support to anyone going through similar experiences as yours - contributing positively can help redefine who you are both in others' eyes as well as in your own.

Make no mistake about it; having a criminal record should not diminish either your worth or potential for growth. Remember, though: with every action comes power to overcome social stigmas and rediscover who you truly are despite past offenses. Take pride in self-acceptance while dedicating to personal growth through supportive networks - your past is no predictor of your future! As we travel this journey together to reclaim power over fulfilling lives.

Guidance on how to overcome stigma, embrace personal development and foster positive self-image is available here.

Today we will examine how we can overcome stigma, embrace personal growth and cultivate positive self-image. I offer my guidance with empathy and wisdom as a life coach who has gone through prison themselves - opening doors towards an optimistic future filled with acceptance, growth and an improved self-image.

Overcoming Stigma

1. **Self-Compassion:** Give yourself kindness and forgiveness while realizing that past events do not determine your worth or potential. Embark upon self-acceptance as the foundation to break free of stigmatized environments and take back power over yourself.

Self-compassion refers to treating oneself with kindness, understanding and empathy. It involves acknowledging suffering, mistakes and imperfections without judgment or self-criticism; cultivating it can serve as an avenue towards personal growth and healing after criminal convictions.

Make no judgment of yourself: Accept that we all make mistakes and that your past doesn't define who you are today. Understand your actions were caused by circumstances in your life and that there's always potential for growth and change ahead. Let go of any weighty self-judgment and embrace change for what it can offer your transformation!

Practice Forgiveness: Forgiveness is an indispensable means of healing and moving on in life, including forgiving oneself of mistakes made or harm caused. Realize that as an adult you've changed and are capable of learning from past errors as well as amends being made now; let forgiveness free you of guilt or self-blame.

Accepting yourself is key to self-compassion and happiness. Recognizing that growth is ongoing is also part of this acceptance. By adopting self-acceptance you will build healthier relationships with yourself while cultivating positive images for yourself.

Consider prioritizing self-care an act of kindness toward yourself. Engage in activities that nourish mind, body, and soul such as exercise, mediation, journaling, spending time in nature or enjoying hobbies which bring pleasure - any activity which improves well being is an act of love and care for oneself! Taking good care of one's well being shows kindness toward themselves.

Attract support: Enlist the assistance of friends, family and community that understand and accept you. Seek advice from life coaches, therapists or support groups with experience helping those with criminal records navigate stigma while building self-compassion.

Strive to eliminate negative self-talk: Tune into the inner dialogue of yourself and challenge any self-criticism or judgment by replacing these statements with positive, affirming ones that focus on strengths, resilience and the progress you have made over time. Be kind and understanding with yourself just like any loved one would expect of them!

Celebrate Progress: Acknowledge and commemorate each step on your personal development journey by acknowledging and celebrating each success along the way. Remember how far you've come and the challenges you have overcome by marking each achievement; by honoring this success you reinforce confidence in your ability to continue growing and evolving over time.

Self-compassion should not mean making excuses for past actions or dismissing their consequences; rather, it means acknowledging your inherent worth, accepting your capacity to grow and choosing to move forward with self-love and understanding. By showing kindness towards yourself, self-compassion will enable you to break free of stigmatized attitudes toward you while creating a future filled with personal fulfillment and acceptance of self.

Knowledge can be an empowering force when it comes to dispelling misconceptions and confronting stereotyping in society. Educating yourself about your rights, laws and available resources can go far towards combatting stigmatism while advocating for change.

By becoming knowledgeable of legal systems and rights of yours as an individual you will empower yourself as you navigate reintegration processes back into society more smoothly - you may even become an advocate for criminal justice reform by breaking down barriers for other who face similar struggles!

Understand Your Rights: Spend some time familiarizing yourself with your rights as someone with a criminal history, from those during arrest and trial through to when reentering society. Knowledge of these rights empowers individuals with criminal records to make more informed decisions, protect themselves against discrimination and ensure fair treatment of themselves and others.

Research the Law: To delve deeply into the legal landscape and examine laws affecting those with criminal histories. Gain familiarity with any laws impacting employment, housing or education as they could impact on reintegration efforts; once aware of such legislation you can effectively advocate for your rights or challenge any discriminatory practices that arise.

Make Use of Available Resources: Take steps to access resources which will aid your reintegration efforts, such as organizations, programs or services that offer assistance with employment, housing, education or counseling services - this way increasing your odds for successful reintegration and personal growth.

Maintain an awareness: Stay abreast of current events and developments within the criminal justice system by staying abreast of news, research, discussions related to reforming policies or initiatives related to justice reform - news articles or research relating to this can provide you with deeper knowledge of challenges experienced by individuals with criminal records as well as pinpoint areas that require change.

Advocate for Reform: Leverage your knowledge and personal experience to become an advocate for criminal justice reform. Share your story to raise awareness about issues faced by people with criminal records; engage in conversations; participate in community initiatives; or support organizations working toward reform by raising your voice - you could make an incredible difference towards breaking down barriers and encouraging social change!

Support and mentor others: Reach out and offer your assistance to others facing similar obstacles, sharing knowledge, experiences and resources to ease the reintegration process for them. Consider volunteering or mentorship roles within organizations providing assistance for people with criminal histories - it will have an amazing impactful difference to someone's journey!

Collaborate with organizations and policymakers: Get involved with organizations and policymakers involved with criminal justice reform by sharing your insights, experiences and suggestions for improvement. Join together with like-minded individuals and groups in advocating for fairer policies that reduce recidivism rates while creating an inclusive society.

Remind yourself that change requires both hard work and collective efforts to implement successfully. Through education, advocacy for reform, and supporting others you are creating an opportunity to shape a juster society with equal access for all. Your personal knowledge can act as powerful catalysts towards breaking down barriers that stand in the way.

Accumulate Support: Seek out people who recognize your potential and offer unflinching encouragement, such as support groups, mentors or life coaches who provide guidance and motivation. By surrounding yourself with positive and understanding relationships you can overcome isolation and build resilience.

Accepting Personal Development: Embark On An Explorative Journey

1. **Reflect and Learn:** Reflection can be an eye-opening and enriching process that allows you to gain new perspectives, learn from past errors, and open yourself up for personal growth. By acknowledging both their failures as well as lessons they brought forward, reflection provides the basis for positive change within yourself and can become a catalyst for personal development. Here's how deepening reflection can serve as a driving force of personal change:

Create a Safe Space for Reflection: Find an isolated yet comfortable spot, such as an area in your home, park or any place which allows for deep reflection without interruptions from outside distractions. Mindful techniques like deep breathing or meditation could help ground and center both thoughts and emotions during reflection time.

Accept self-honesty: Conduct an honest, nonjudgmental examination of past experiences, with particular focus on errors that occurred due to your actions (taking responsibility without dwelling in guilt or shame), mistakes you've made in relation to these, mistakes you regret having committed and mistakes caused due to indecision on part of others (making mistakes without dwelling on guilt and shame), being open and vulnerable in order to foster meaningful personal growth.

As you reflect, identify lessons and growth opportunities: When reflecting upon past experiences, focus on what lessons have been gained from challenging encounters; what insights did these encounters yield; how have these encounters altered values, beliefs, or aspirations; search for patterns or themes or areas for improvement to provide yourself a roadmap towards personal development. This self-awareness journey should lead to personal transformation journey.

Set Specific and Achievable Goals: Take your insights gained through reflection to set specific and achievable goals that reflect both your values and aspirations. Your SMART goals (specific, measurable, attainable, relevant, time bound goals) should provide actionable steps that move closer towards realizing desired results and giving yourself clear direction and sense of purpose. By setting clear goals you give yourself direction and purposeful living!

Cultivate a growth mindset: Adopting a growth mindset means acknowledging that both your abilities and intelligence can be improved with dedication, effort, and ongoing learning. Recognize setbacks as opportunities to push yourself farther along your journey while viewing challenges as steps rather than roadblocks; when adopting such an outlook you open yourself up to new possibilities while dismantling self-limiting beliefs that might limit or confine you.

Seek Feedback and Support: Don't be shy to solicit input from trusted members in your life for guidance, insights, or support on your personal growth journey. Their insights may provide important viewpoints. Surround yourself with supportive friends, family members, mentors or life coaches who can offer guidance, encouragement, accountability on this path towards greater personal fulfillment.

Self-Reflection Should Be Done Regularly: Reflection shouldn't just be limited to an isolated moment but should become part of your everyday practice. Set aside regular times for personal reflection so you can track your progress, review goals and adapt course if necessary. Journaling can also serve as an invaluable method for self-reflection by helping document thoughts, emotions and observations in one convenient place.

Personal growth is a life-long pursuit that demands patience, perseverance, and an unyielding dedication to self-improvement. Through reflecting upon past experiences, taking note of any mistakes, and understanding lessons learned can pave the path toward living a more rewarding, purpose-driven lifestyle in accordance with values and aspirations. Each step towards personal development brings you one step closer towards creating your ideal life!

2. **Acquire Knowledge and Skills**: Leaping into knowledge acquisition can be transformative on your personal growth journey, whether formal education, vocational training, or self-directed learning is involved. Making time to acquire new skills has an enormously positive effect on one's self-esteem as it opens doors to endless new opportunities - here's why and how education and skill acquisition should play an integral part of that equation:

Enhancing Self-Confidence: Acquiring new knowledge and abilities builds your competence and self-assurance. As you acquire expertise in one field or learn a new one, your confidence increases accordingly, impacting multiple areas of life from career searches to social engagements.

Enhancing Opportunities: Education and skill acquisition provide invaluable ways of broadening horizons and broadening options. By investing in your personal development, investing in yourself increases marketability and the possibility of accessing higher-paying jobs or entrepreneurial endeavors. Furthermore, learning new skills may open doors that were previously closed off to you so you can pursue passions or interests more freely than before.

Remain relevant by staying abreast of changing industries: To remain successful in today's ever-evolving environment, constant learning is vitally important in order to stay on the cutting edge. Industries and job markets constantly change and developing new skills will enable you to adapt. By remaining up-to-date with trends and advancements, staying informed increases both employability and career advancement potential.

Personal Fulfillment and Growth: Education is not solely focused on professional advancement; rather it provides personal fulfillment and growth by broadening knowledge bases, broadening perspectives, and stretching intellectual capacity. Discovering new subjects or fields or cultivating hobbies may bring joy, fulfillment and greater comprehension of how the world functions around us.

Pursuing higher education: Pursuing higher education can provide comprehensive knowledge and advanced certifications in specific fields, equipping you with critical thinking abilities, research techniques and an expanded perspective of social issues. Furthermore, higher education offers networking opportunities as well as resources which will support both personal and professional growth.

Vocational Training and Skill-Specific Certifications: Vocational training programs and certifications offer practical, hands-on learning experiences designed to equip individuals with the required knowledge, skills, and abilities necessary for specific industries or trades. Vocations training may include plumbing, carpentry, healthcare or information technology-focused certification programs with rewarding careers with strong earning potentials.

Self-Directed Learning: Self-directed learning enables you to tailor your educational journey based on your own interests and goals, whether that means reading books, taking online courses, attending workshops or webinars - or any combination thereof! With today's abundance of educational platforms and resources online learning platforms offer today, this form of education allows for flexibility when choosing what, when, and how much knowledge to acquire for personal growth purposes based on self-direction learning platforms available today allowing personal control over personal growth goals by tapping into knowledge that spark passion in them.

Education and skill acquisition is a lifelong pursuit that should be approached with curiosity, openness and an optimistic growth mindset. Seek opportunities for personal development whether through formal education programs, vocational training courses or self-directed study. By continuously broadening your knowledge and abilities you equip yourself to seize new opportunities, adapt to changes in society more readily, and experience personal fulfillment on the road of self-discovery and growth.

3. **View Challenges as Opportunities:** Adopting the mindset that sees challenges as opportunities rather than impediments is one way you can boost personal development and overcome hardships more efficiently. By shifting perspective and accepting challenges as chances

for personal transformation, you cultivate resilience, develop character traits, and can unlock their full potential to drive lasting change within yourself and society at large. Here is how this mindset can benefit your growth:

Accept a Growth Mindset: Adopt a growth mindset, which recognizes challenges as opportunities to learn and advance your development. Instead of viewing setbacks as failures or roadblocks, embrace them as valuable experiences which strengthen resilience and character building. Adopt the belief that with effort, perseverance, and learning behind you you can overcome any challenge to continue growing and evolving as an individual.

Cultivate Resilience: Resilience refers to your capacity for recovery after setbacks or change and to thrive despite challenges. By seeing obstacles as opportunities, resilience can be developed through perseverance and finding creative solutions in times of trouble - each hurdle you overcome strengthens it further and shows your ability to confront future ones with confidence.

Seize Learning and Growth Opportunities: View each experience as an opportunity for personal and professional growth. Take stock of what lessons can be gleaned from challenging circumstances; what skills did you develop, insights gained or ways did your growth progress. By actively searching out these insights you'll discover value even from difficult circumstances.

Develop Your Problem-Solving Skills: Challenges are opportunities for problem-solving and innovation, rather than obstacles that obstruct progress. Instead of becoming discouraged or becoming overwhelmed when confronted by difficulties, view challenges with an optimistic, solutions-oriented outlook: break your problem down into smaller, manageable tasks; brainstorm possible solutions; then take appropriate actions - the more problem-solving practiced one gets the more adept you become at finding creative approaches to surmount obstacles!

Accept a Learning Mindset: Take on a mindset of lifelong learning where every experience provides opportunities to acquire new knowledge, skills, and perspectives. Look upon challenges as opportunities to expand capabilities and broaden understanding while approaching each situation with curiosity while asking questions that provoke deeper reflection on its lessons. By adopting such an outlook you create an endless cycle of personal transformation and expansion.

Practice self-reflection: Reflect frequently on your experiences, challenges and lessons from life so far. Self-reflection can provide deep insights into your strengths, areas for development and progress made over time - helping identify patterns, identify strategies that work and adjust approaches when necessary; ultimately leading to self-awareness and driving forward personal development.

Celebrate Progress and Accomplishments: Acknowledge and celebrate any advancement or successes, no matter how small. Recognize efforts you made towards overcoming challenges and experiencing growth; celebrating milestones will strengthen the belief in yourself to navigate future obstacles as well as remind you of all you've accomplished on your personal growth journey.

Do not underestimate challenges as an opportunity, rather see them as catalysts of progress and transformation in your life. By accepting them as catalysts of transformation you can build one filled with growth, fulfillment, and success. Affronts to life can often present themselves to us all and our response to them can have profound effects on personal development; yet challenges should not define us but instead serve as powerful catalysts of personal change and personal transformation.

Accept them as opportunities for personal growth, resilience building and transformative experiences. By cultivating a growth mindset and welcoming learning as part of self-reflection practice, you will find more grace to face your challenges with ease while seizing any opportunity that presents itself for continuous personal development.

By viewing challenges as opportunities, rather than as obstacles, we can navigate them more successfully and seize any opportunity for personal development that arises - creating an ongoing path of continuous self-improvement and progress.

Cultivating a Positive Self-Image:

1. **Engage in Self-Care:** Prioritizing self-care on the journey towards reentry is vitally important; it serves to reclaim identity, restore balance, and move beyond any

challenges encountered along the way. Having been through my own experience as an inmate myself, I know the burden incarceration places upon one's sense of worthiness and wellbeing - therefore prioritizing self-care practices should not be seen as selfish but as essential steps toward rebuilding positive self-image and creating an optimistic outlook towards creating an optimistic future!

Physical self-care involves taking good care in caring for yourself by engaging in activities that promote physical wellbeing, such as regular physical activities such as walking, jogging and sports participation. Physical activities not only boost physical fitness but they can also release endorphins that boost mood and lower stress. Furthermore, paying attention to nutrition by selecting healthy food options provides your body with energy for growth and nourishment that it requires for survival.

Emotional self-care entails understanding and accepting your emotions while making sure to express and process them in healthy ways. It is key to create a safe space where reflection, journaling or other therapeutic activities may promote healing - this may involve seeking support from trusted individuals such as friends, family or mentors who understand and acknowledge your experiences - connecting with like minded peers can give an incredible sense of community support; reminding us we're not alone on our journeys.

Mental self-care involves prioritizing activities that stimulate and nourish your mind, such as reading books or listening to educational podcasts; learning new skills; or exploring creative outlets like art, music or writing. Engaging in such mental stimulation activities will strengthen cognitive abilities while building self-confidence and widening perspectives on life.

Implementing self-care practices into your everyday routine is critical to leading a fulfilling, healthful lifestyle. Here are some proven techniques:

Build Your Self-Care Routine: Establish an ongoing self-care routine: set aside specific times every day or week specifically for self-care activities and prioritize it as part of everyday living.

Explore Different Self-Care Activities: Find what brings joy and peace for you by trying different self-care activities. It may include practicing mindfulness, engaging in hobbies, taking a relaxing bath or spending time in nature - find what resonates and make it part of your regular routine!

Practice Self-Compassion: Be kind to yourself by practicing self-compassion. Recognize that you deserve care, understanding, and forgiveness from yourself as part of life's journey of discovery - instead focusing on perceived setbacks! Embark upon it without shame or blame as progress rather than perceived setbacks is what matters!

Setting Boundaries: Create boundaries to protect your time, energy, and wellbeing. Learn to decline activities that drain you while prioritizing those which uphold and nurture.

Seek Support: Connect with community organizations, support groups or professional counseling services where you can share experiences, receive guidance and connect with like-minded people who offer insight and offer essential help and assistance.

Self-care should be part of an ongoing journey and may evolve over time as you reenter society. By nurturing your physical, emotional and mental well-being you're taking proactive steps toward rebuilding a positive self-image - so embrace self-care as an act of love towards yourself; give yourself time and space to heal beyond incarceration! Your well being deserves this time to blossom!

2. **Positive Affirmations:** Attuned to the transformative powers of positive self-talk as both an ex-incarcerated individual and life coach, I understand its remarkable effect on mindsets and overall well-being. Embracing positive self-talk allows one to shift away from doubtful or negative thoughts towards affirmations that uplift and inspire - creating an upbeat self image by reinforcing strengths, resilience and acknowledging progress made over time.

Positive self-talk involves deliberately replacing self-limiting beliefs with positive and uplifting ones, acting as your own cheerleader and speaking with kindness, compassion, and belief in your ability for transformation. Below are a few strategies for harnessing its power:

To Recognize and Confront Negative Thoughts: Begin by becoming mindful of any self-critical talk that arises. Pay close attention when self-doubt or negative emotions appear within yourself or externally from others, then question their validity by replacing these statements with positive affirming statements.

Make Your Own Affirmations: Generate personalized affirmations statements that address the journey and goals that resonate with you and reflect positively upon them, like "I am resilient and capable of meeting any challenge", and/or "I deserve success and happiness in my life".

Apply Daily Affirmations: Make affirmations part of your everyday practice. Set aside dedicated time each day to repeat these affirmations out loud or write them out and speak them sincerely with conviction as though you believe their truth; over time these will rewire your mindset and build positive self-images.

Fill Your Environment With Positive Influences: Be conscious of who and what influences are part of your environment, such as people and media you consume or are exposed to. Befriend individuals who uplift and inspire you, as well as content which promotes positivity, personal growth, resilience and positivity - this will create a supportive atmosphere which strengthens positive self-talk.

Recognizing Your Progress: Take time to acknowledge and celebrate the progress made during your reentry journey. Take note of even small achievements, no matter how insignificant they might seem; recognize steps taken and positive changes implemented - doing this will reinforce a sense of achievement while building self-confidence.

Cultivate Self-Compassion: Be gentle and kind towards yourself during this process. Reappoint setbacks as inevitable elements of life; practice self-compassion by offering understanding, forgiveness and support - treat yourself the way you would treat a close friend or loved one.

Harnessing the power of positive self-talk is an empowering practice that can transform your mindset, boost confidence, and guide your reentry journey forward. By replacing self-doubt and negative thoughts with affirmations of inspiration and upliftment, positive self-talk provides you with a tool to reshape your image of self and reinforce belief in your capacity for change - an empowering practice which could propel you toward living an abundant and successful life outside incarceration - with positive self-talk supporting you every step of the way!

3. **Celebrate Your Unique Journey and Authenticity:** Be proud of the unique path and authenticity that defines you, but never allow past experiences to define who you are today. Share your story when the time is right; sharing will inspire others while dispelling stigma along the way.

My courageous friends, remember that personal development is an ongoing journey of transformation and discovery. Tackling stigma begins with self-compassion but must extend further - including advocating for change while informing and educating others about it. Unleashing personal development involves reflection, seeking knowledge, and accepting challenges with grace. Nurturing positive self-image through self-care practices such as positive affirmations is also crucial - don't hide from who you really are! Your story matters and so do its outcomes; now is your opportunity to rewrite yours by building an affirmative self-image for tomorrow. Join me as we embark upon this transformative journey together - supporting each other along this path towards growth! Your potential knows no boundaries - let's seize it now.

The importance of personal narratives and challenging societal stereotypes

My time behind bars allowed me to witness first-hand the power of personal narratives and their effects on society's stereotypes, including gendered roles and stigmatized cultures. Let us embark on this chapter's journey of self-discovery, resilience and truth together!

Societal Stereotypes and Incarceration: Society's stereotypes surrounding imprisonment cast an unwanted shadow over people with criminal records. Such stereotyping hinders reintegration efforts and limits opportunities for growth; further reinforcing marginalization cycles while undermining personal growth - reinforcing that their past dictates their future and reinforcing stereotypes that dictate those lives as though their past determines everything about who they are today. Now is the time to challenge and redefine such narratives!

Reclaiming Personal Narratives: Our individual narratives hold immense power; they define who we are as individuals, our self-perception, and how others see us. Embracing these stories gives us agency over our past mistakes while showing the fullness of life beyond "incarcerated". Stories may inspire change while challenging preconceptions within society.

Breaking Free From Victimhood: Individuals who have had experience of imprisonment may feel they have been cast in a victim role and stripped of agency and potential. It is vitally important that they recognize past experiences without becoming defined solely by them, taking charge of our lives to move beyond any restrictions imposed upon us and develop an sense of empowerment that empowers them as whole persons.

Redefining Success: Society often measures success based on traditional measures like wealth, status and material possessions; however as former inmates we have an opportunity to redefine it on our terms - shifting attention away from wealth accumulation toward personal growth, resilience building and positively contributing to communities - making success the embodiment of transformation, overcoming hardship and living according to personal values.

Michael A. Davis

Advocating for Change: Challenging stereotypes requires collaborative efforts. By sharing our experiences and advocating for criminal justice reform, we become agents of change. Through advocacy we promote empathy, understanding, and an inclusive society.

Inspiration of Others: Our stories can motivate and empower others who are experiencing similar issues. By openly sharing them, our experiences give others hope that change is possible and show that one's criminal past does not determine worth or potential. Through mentorship programs, support groups, community engagement activities, we can uphold individuals on their individual journeys of transformation and self-discovery.

Life should not limit us. By challenging societal stereotypes and crafting inspiring narratives of our own lives, we reclaim our identities, embrace personal development and reduce stigmatism. Together we can rewrite the narrative around incarceration to foster more compassionate and inclusive societies; let us become authors of our own stories so as not to become victims of past errors but instead celebrated for showing resilience, transformation and our unbreakable human potential!

Chapter 6

Mental Health and Well-being

Examining the prevalence of mental health concerns among individuals transitioning back into society from imprisonment

Transitioning back into society after time behind bars is no simple journey, and mental health concerns must be taken into consideration during this process. I know first-hand the unique difficulties experienced as individuals reintegrate back into society - let's approach this topic together, with empathy and an emphasis on personal growth and well-being!

Many individuals incarcerated suffer from various mental health disorders, including anxiety, depression, post-traumatic stress disorder (PTSD), substance use disorders and more. Incarceration itself may be traumatizing enough to increase or deepen any existing mental health concerns while stigma and social isolation often associated with criminal records can exacerbate mental health concerns further.

As a life coach, I recognize the significance of self-reflection and improvement for personal wellbeing. Recognizing mental health conditions as natural responses to challenging circumstances is vitally important during transition processes; encouraging individuals to seek support is also essential in prioritizing wellbeing during this journey.

As part of my life coaching practice, my aim is to foster an environment conducive to mental wellness that's supportive and nonjudgmental. Through dialogue and active listening sessions, open dialogue provides individuals a safe space in which they can express their emotions freely while sharing experiences from life. By cultivating empathy, understanding, and compassion during this process.

Support systems play a pivotal role in helping individuals transition successfully, connecting individuals with resources like therapy, support groups, and community organizations that specialize in reentry can prove invaluable in providing invaluable help for successful reentry. Utilizing such resources will equip individuals to develop effective coping mechanisms, foster resilience and acquire necessary skills that enable them to successfully face any future obstacles that they might come across.

Promote self-care practices are integral for mental wellbeing. Encouraging individuals to engage in activities they enjoy, practice mindfulness regularly and prioritizing healthy relationships can all make an important impactful contribution toward emotional and mental well-being. Offering guidance for stress management techniques as well as setting manageable goals may further help people in rebuilding their lives.

As a life coach, my role is to assist individuals on their personal growth journey by emphasizing empowerment and resilience. Recognizing mental health issues with empathy will assist individuals transitioning back into society after time behind bars thrive in their new lives and reduce stigma surrounding mental illness thereby creating more inclusive communities.

Explore barriers to mental health services and identify strategies for meeting mental health needs.

Accessing mental health services may prove challenging for various populations due to various barriers. Let's examine these hurdles, along with strategies and sources of support available for meeting mental health needs.

1. Financial Barriers:

Lack of Insurance Coverage: Many individuals face obstacles related to insufficient or no insurance coverage for mental health services. Strategies include expanding Medicaid, implementing the Affordable Care Act (ACA), and upholding parity laws to guarantee equitable coverage of mental health services (Source: Substance Abuse and Mental Health Services Administration [SAMHSA].)

2. Stigma and Discrimination:

Stigmatized mental health conditions often discourage individuals from seeking assistance and contribute to disparate accessing care for all those afflicted.

Strategies such as public education campaigns, anti-stigma programs and culturally competent services promotion may reduce stigmatization of mental health support while simultaneously increasing acceptance for such support (Source: World Health Organization [WHO]). (

3. Lack of Awareness and Knowledge: Individuals may not know of available mental health services and how to access them, leaving them unaware. Strategies include community outreach and education initiatives, using technology for information dissemination purposes, providing culturally sensitive resources (Source: SAMHSA).

4. Shortage of Mental Health Providers: A shortage of mental health providers in rural or underserved areas can significantly restrict access to necessary treatment and can make care harder to come by. Strategies include expanding the mental health workforce through recruitment and retention efforts, offering financial incentives for providers practicing in underserved areas, and offering telehealth services that reach remote populations (source: National Institute of Mental Health [NIMH]). (NIMH).

5. Systemic and Structural Barriers:Systemic issues, including fragmented care, complex referral processes and lack of coordination across agencies can inhibit access to

mental health services. These strategies, supported by empirical research and recommendations from organizations like SAMHSA, WHO, NIMH and OMH, aim to reduce barriers and enhance access to mental health services. By eliminating such obstructions we can increase mental wellbeing support as a collective whole while leading towards overall well-being for all individuals involved.

Highlight the importance of self-care, resilience and seeking support

As someone who was previously incarcerated, I wish to emphasize the critical significance of self-care, resilience, and seeking support during our transition back into society. From my personal experience I know first-hand of all the difficulties associated with doing this work - these practices make a powerful impact in lives today!

Self-care is not selfish; it is an act of love for yourself and others. By prioritizing our physical, emotional and mental wellness we create the basis of a healthier and more satisfying lifestyle. Engaging in activities designed for self-care helps recharge us to manage stress effectively as well as cultivate positivity - such as taking walks in nature or practicing meditation; practicing hobbies or spending quality time with loved ones can all serve to foster balance within us while strengthening resilience during challenging periods and maintaining overall well-being. By including it regularly in our routine self care strengthens resilience while strengthening overall well being and maintaining its overall well being.

Resilience is the inner strength that allows us to overcome difficulties and keep moving forward, even during times of trouble and difficulty. Transitioning back into society after imprisonment is no small task: there may be obstacles like finding employment and housing stability as well as rebuilding relationships or combatting stigmatism - yet resilience allows us to navigate these hurdles and emerge stronger than before - through cultivating growth mindset beliefs about our ability to overcome obstacles as well as viewing setbacks as opportunities for personal development and tapping into innate resources of adapting, learning, and flourishing when life gets difficult or challenging!

Seeking support does not constitute weakness but instead represents an essential step toward growth and healing. Sometimes the journey from prison can feel isolating as we grapple with both past trauma and judgment from outsiders. Reaching out for help can provide us with invaluable guidance, encouragement and resources - such as from friends, family members, mentors, support groups or professionals in mental health fields. Sharing our struggles with others allows us to relieve some of our burdens while discovering fresh perspectives and renewing hope. Being supported creates a safety net which empowers us to meet challenges more resiliently with optimism.

On my personal journey, I have witnessed first-hand the transformative powers of self-care practices, resilience development and seeking support. By engaging in self-care practices I learned how to prioritize my wellbeing while discovering activities which brought joy and peace; by developing resilience I turned setbacks into opportunities for growth while developing confidence that any obstacle could be surmounted; while by seeking support I found an understanding community who provided guidance, empathy, and unwavering assistance on my journey back into society.

Individuals transitioning back into society after time in prison should prioritize self-care, resilience and the courage to ask for support. We each possess the power within us to rebuild our lives, pursue our goals, and contribute meaningfully to society - let's prioritize well-being while cultivating inner strength through community support - we can rewrite narratives, end recidivism cycles and inspire positive transformation together!

Remember, your past does not define you. While the journey ahead may prove challenging, with proper self-care, resilience and support systems in place you possess the power to craft an optimistic and fulfilling future - one filled with hope, purpose, and endless potentialities. So embrace these practices, trust yourself and know that self-improvement practices such as resilience building will allow you to transform your life beyond anything imagined - the destination is worth every step taken on this path! I stand beside you as evidence of their transformative powers! You are never alone: I stand here as witness to their transformative power!

Michael A. Davis

As one embarks upon their transition back into society from imprisonment, it's vitally important to bear in mind the long and often difficult journey ahead may be difficult and daunting. Our past mistakes can weigh heavy on us; social barriers may obstruct our path forward but during these moments it is vitally important that we hold onto hope that every step we take leads towards something worthwhile - our destination justifies each one!

Destiny of our life should be one filled with fulfilment, purpose and positive contributions to society. In such a life we have the chance to rewrite our narratives, break free of past burdens and shape a brighter future - where errors do not define but rather serve as tools towards personal transformation and development.

As we journey together through life's trials and tribulations, it's crucial that we remember we're never alone. Others have come before us on this path with similar struggles and obstacles; I stand ready to offer support, encouragement and understanding on your behalf as someone who was once imprisoned herself - I understand first-hand both your challenges and strengths that exist within you!

Self-care can be an invaluable aid on our journeys. By prioritizing our well-being, we can improve physical, emotional, and mental wellbeing. Engaging in activities designed for self-care can recharge our energy reserves while simultaneously relieving stress. Engaging in activities designed specifically to take care of us provides enjoyment, peace, and fulfillment; finding activities such as taking a bath, reading a book, practicing mindfulness meditation techniques or engaging in creative pursuits may all play an integral part of self-care as a reminder that love, kindness, healing are due us!

Resilience is what keeps us moving forward despite setbacks and challenges, helping us overcome them with courage, adaptability and unwavering hope. Resilience allows us to rebound quickly after experiencing hardship, learn from past errors and continue with determination on our journeys. Developing resilience involves cultivating a growth mindset, accepting change as opportunities for personal development, viewing obstacles as challenges rather than obstacles in terms of growth potential, believing in ourselves when facing challenging times as it helps strengthen us physically as well. Resilience allows us to face difficulties head on while keeping hope alive through resilience despite setbacks by giving rise to courage adaptability & unwavering hope!

Establishing and seeking support are acts of courage and vulnerability; they serve to acknowledge that we cannot navigate life alone, with individuals and communities offering guidance, empathy, resources and emotional support in various forms. Reaching out can bring relief; reach out to trusted friends, family or mentors can offer encouragement or understanding while joining support groups or engaging in therapy or counseling will provide professional assistance as needed. Having people care for our success and wellbeing creates a safety net reiterating this fact.

Collectively, through self-care, resilience, and seeking support we can bring lasting change to ourselves and to the communities in which we reside. Every step we take - no matter how small - brings us closer towards reaching the destination we envision for ourselves; so it is crucial that we celebrate each step we take along the way and be kind and patient with ourselves on this journey of self-discovery. Every step along our journey counts and I stand beside you as proof of self-care's transformative powers as you find your footing again in society. Trust in your strengths; remember the incredible potential within.

Chapter 7

Advocating for Criminal Justice Reform

Disseminate information regarding systemic changes needed to assist successful reentry and reduce recidivism

As part of our quest for social justice and equality, the need for systemic changes that facilitate successful reentry and reduce recidivism are of utmost importance. Unfortunately, our current criminal justice system is plagued with inequities that prolong cycles of imprisonment while impeding individuals' efforts at reintegrating back into society. I am passionate about combatting these systemic issues while advocating for transformative reforms which promote rehabilitation, equality and equal treatment of all.

One key component of successful reentry involves providing individuals with access to essential resources that allow them to rebuild their lives after imprisonment, such as affordable housing, employment opportunities, educational and healthcare services. Unfortunately, former inmates often face challenges accessing such essential services due to systemic barriers or societal biases that prevent access.

To address this challenge, we must advocate for policies which remove barriers and promote equal opportunities for those transitioning back into society following imprisonment. This may require changing laws which restrict housing, employment and educational access based solely on criminal records; adopting fair chance hiring practices which give individuals with criminal backgrounds real chances to rebuild their lives through gainful employment; as well as expanding education and vocational training programs so all individuals have equal access to obtain skills necessary to secure stable jobs that contribute meaningfully back into society.

As part of any effective solution to recidivism, our current criminal justice system must shift focus from punishment to rehabilitation. Punitive measures often only serve to prolong cycles of imprisonment rather than provide individuals with tools they require for successful reintegration back into society. It's imperative that comprehensive and evidence-based rehabilitation programs within correctional facilities address factors underlying criminality such as substance abuse, mental health concerns or lack of job skills - so as to successfully combat recidivism.

Furthermore, we must promote restorative justice practices that prioritize healing and accountability over retribution. Restorative justice allows individuals to take responsibility for their actions, make reparations to victims or communities when harm has been caused and engage in meaningful dialogue and reconciliation efforts with these same efforts within our criminal justice system. By adopting restorative justice principles within criminal law systems around the country we can create more humane and transformative systems of justice which promote healing while decreasing recidivism rates.

Furthermore, we must address racial and socioeconomic disparities within the criminal justice system. Marginalized communities - specifically communities of color - are particularly impacted by mass incarceration, with further barriers posed upon release into society after release from incarceration. To achieve social justice, we must actively work toward dismantling systemic biases within criminal justice processes so all individuals regardless of background receive equitable treatment throughout.

Advocating for systemic changes requires challenging the profit-driven nature of the prison-industrial complex. Private prisons and other entities that profit from mass incarceration perpetuate an system that prioritizes filling beds over rehabilitation and public safety; we must fight to abolish private prisons while reallocating resources towards community-based alternatives that prioritize prevention, diversion, and restorative justice practices.

Michael A. Davis

As an active social justice activist, I firmly believe that successfully reentering society and reducing recidivism require holistic systemic changes. Simply looking at individual cases won't do; we must examine and transform systems and structures which perpetuate cycles of imprisonment as a part of creating an environment conducive to successful reentry and break the cycle of recidivism. By tackling root causes while making wide scale system changes we can foster individuals in their reintegration journey while breaking free of repeat convictions.

1. Education and Employment Opportunities: Education and employment access is central to successful reentry, so addressing any obstacles that prevent people with criminal backgrounds from finding meaningful work or education opportunities must be prioritized. Advocating for fair hiring practices, promoting vocational training programs, expanding access to higher education for these individuals are among the ways in which we empower individuals with criminal records to lead fulfilling lives while decreasing recidivism rates. By opening up paths towards education and employment we empower people to create stable lives free of criminal convictions thus decreasing likelihood of recidivism and recidivism rates overall.

2. Access to Housing: Stable housing is integral for successful reentry as it offers stability, belonging, and provides the foundation upon which one can rebuild one's life. However, individuals with criminal records often encounter difficulty securing such accommodations due to discriminatory practices and restrictions; it is therefore

crucial that advocates for fair housing policies that prohibit discriminatory practices against criminal record holders while expanding affordable options available to people reentering society - secure housing supports not only successful reintegration efforts but also reduces homelessness risk as well as involvement with criminal justice institutions.

3. Mental Health and Substance Abuse Treatment: Many individuals leaving prison often struggle with mental health and substance use disorders that impede successful reentry, so in order to aid a smooth process we need accessible and quality mental health and substance abuse programs available - investments in community mental health services, accessing evidence-based treatments options, as well as including mental healthcare in the reentry process can make an enormous difference and decrease rates of recidivism dramatically.

4. Community Reintegration Programs: Successful reentry requires creating an environment conducive to rehabilitation, reduced stigmatization and offered resources to individuals transitioning out of incarceration. Investing in community organizations providing these vital reintegration services as they offer counseling, life skills training, job placement assistance as well as support networks can create the conditions needed for people to flourish successfully reenter society after serving time. By cultivating the sense of community support we create conditions necessary for individuals reenter successfully into society and establish the conditions necessary for them

reentering society successfully reentering society successfully reentry is ensured and successful reentry is created allowing for successful reentry back into society.

5. Sentencing and Criminal Justice Reform: System-wide changes must take place to reduce incarceration's overuse while encouraging rehabilitation through alternative solutions that emphasize community support systems and rehabilitation services. These may include advocating for sentencing reform, diversion programs, restorative justice practices and increased investments in community resources as means to shift our emphasis from punishment towards rehabilitation; providing individuals with tools they require for successful reentry to society after release from incarceration.

6. Address Racial and Socioeconomic Disparities: The criminal justice system often impacts marginalized communities disproportionately, exacerbating existing racial and socioeconomic inequalities. To facilitate successful reentry and reduce recidivism rates, we must address systemic inequities by challenging discriminatory practices, advocating for equitable policies, promoting racial and economic equity and dismantling systemic barriers; by doing so we create an equal society which embraces all individuals on their journey back.

7. Collaboration and Coordination: Addressing reentry and recidivism requires collaboration and coordination across many stakeholders - government agencies, community organizations, service providers, individuals with

lived experience as well as individuals from lived experience themselves. Partnerships that foster information sharing, coordination of services and evidence-based practices must also be developed in order to form cohesive support systems which increase chances of successful reintegration into society.

Conclusion. Achieving successful reentry and reducing recidivism requires systemic changes that extend far beyond individual efforts. By advocating for education and employment opportunities, access to housing, mental health and substance abuse treatment services, community support services for reintegration programs and sentencing reform, as well as addressing disparities, we can create an enabling society that aids individuals on their path toward successful reintegration. These systemic changes aim at making society more just and equitable thereby breaking cycles of recidivism while offering individuals an opportunity to rebuild lives while contributing positively towards community life.

Explore policy initiatives, community-based alternatives and restorative justice approaches.

As someone who has directly experienced incarceration, I want to highlight the significance of policy initiatives, community-based alternatives and restorative justice approaches in revamping criminal justice systems.

Policy Initiatives: Reform is critical for effective crime control measures that prioritize rehabilitation over punishment. Initiatives could include:

1. Sentencing Reform: Reevaluating sentencing guidelines so they are fair and proportionate while prioritizing rehabilitation over incarceration, through community service, probation or restorative justice programs.

2. Reentry Support: Implementing policies that offer comprehensive reentry support services can assist individuals transitioning back into society from imprisonment. These may include access to education, job training, mental health services, substance abuse treatment options and housing support - thus decreasing recidivism rates. By eliminating obstacles to successful reentry we can lower recidivism levels significantly.

3. Bail Reform: Examining the cash bail system that results in pretrial detention for individuals who can't afford bail can prevent pretrial detention solely because they lack money to post bail. Offering alternatives such as risk evaluation and supervised release could prevent individuals being jailed solely due to inability to pay bail.

Community-Based Alternatives: As opposed to solely using incarceration as a response to criminal behavior, community-based alternatives offer more efficient and rehabilitative strategies that address it. Examples may include:

1. Diversion Programs: Diversion programs divert individuals away from criminal justice system by diverting them into community-based programs which address their actions' underlying causes, such as substance abuse treatment or mental health support or restorative justice

practices. These could include substance abuse treatment programs or restorative justice practices as potential solutions.

2. Specialty Courts: Establishing specialty courts such as drug, mental health or veterans courts that offer targeted interventions and treatments tailored to individuals' specific needs can address root causes of criminal behavior while linking individuals with necessary support services.

3. Community Accountability Boards: Establishing community boards that work in cooperation with the justice system to hold individuals responsible for their actions while offering rehabilitation support services is one way of holding individuals accountable while at the same time improving relationships among offenders, community members and their victims. These boards include all affected residents as decision makers while helping restore relationships among offenders, victims and affected parties.

Restorative Justice Approaches: Restorative justice emphasizes repairing any harm done by crimes to both victims and communities alike and seeks to promote true rehabilitation through restorative practices such as:

1. Victim-Offender Mediation: Facilitating dialogues between victims and offenders to express feelings, ask questions, and seek ways to repair harm done is known to facilitate greater understanding, empathy, accountability, as well as meaningful reconciliation.

2. Circle Processes: Engaging individuals involved with the justice system as well as community members in dialogue-focused circles which promote dialogue, active listening and mutual respect can facilitate healing, problem-solving and accountability through taking a more active stance towards taking responsibility for one's actions.

3. Community Reparation: Encouraging offenders to contribute positively to their communities through acts of reparation such as community service or restitution is one way of helping rebuild trust between members, develop new skills and atone for harm done by offender. This method helps individuals reestablish respect while atoning for any wrongs done to others by individuals responsible.

As someone who was once imprisoned, I believe these policy initiatives, community-based alternatives and restorative justice approaches hold great potential to transform the criminal justice system. By prioritizing rehabilitation over punitive measures we can create a more just, effective system focused on helping individuals reintegrate successfully back into society. Let us fight together towards creating this better future where rehabilitation takes precedence over punitive measures.

Encourage readers to become advocates for criminal justice reform.

Becoming an advocate for criminal justice reform can not only support those directly impacted by its effects, but can also make real and long-lasting change within communities. If justice, equality, or rehabilitation is important to you then I encourage you to become an advocate. Here's why your voice matters:

1. Empowerment and Representation: Advocating for criminal justice reform can give voice to those directly impacted by it - including individuals incarcerated themselves - by amplifying their voices through your advocacy work for change. Your involvement helps foster an inclusive movement towards lasting change.

2. Human Rights and Dignity: Advocating for criminal justice reform should always begin from an emphasis on upholding human rights and dignity for everyone, no matter their previous offenses. By advocating for reform you help create a system focused on rehabilitation instead of punishment and stigmatization cycles.

3. Addressing Systemic Injustices: The criminal justice system often disproportionally impacts marginalized communities, creating racial and socioeconomic inequalities. As an advocate, you have the power to address systemic injustices by challenging discriminatory policies or advocating for alternatives to imprisonment such as restorative justice approaches - ultimately working toward creating a fairer system overall.

4. Positive Community Effect: Criminal justice reform has far-reaching ramifications beyond individual lives; its ripples extend deep into our communities and its advocates' advocacy helps build safer and more supportive environments for everyone involved. Rehabilitation-oriented

policies or alternatives to incarceration may reduce recidivism rates while strengthening bonds within local neighborhoods while creating accountability and healing among both offenders and victims of crime.

5. Influencing Policy and Legislation: Advocacy efforts have the power to influence policy and legislative changes. By meeting with elected officials, policymakers, and community leaders you can educate them about reform needs as well as evidence-based practices such as rehabilitation therapies that prioritize rehabilitation, fairness and community well being. Through sharing your personal stories you may also help shape policies which prioritize rehabilitation services as a priority and support community well being.

6. Building Coalitions and Mobilizing Change: Joining forces with like-minded individuals, organizations, and grassroots movements allows for maximum collective impact. By connecting with existing advocacy groups, attending community forums, or attending public hearings you can contribute towards building coalitions and mobilizing change - raising awareness, sparking conversations, or creating momentum towards meaningful reform initiatives.

7. Foster Empathy and Understanding: Through advocacy, you can help promote empathy, understanding, dialogue, and dialogue surrounding the complex criminal justice system. Sharing stories, dispelling myths and humanizing those impacted by incarceration are ways you

can break stereotypes while building an informed society with more compassion for individuals who experience imprisonment.

Remember, advocacy for criminal justice reform doesn't entail only large-scale activities; every effort, no matter how small, makes an impactful difference. From engaging in conversations with family and friends about reform to writing letters to elected officials or attending community meetings dedicated to it - every action contributes towards creating real change!

By joining the community of advocates for criminal justice reform, you join a movement dedicated to building a more just and equitable society. Your advocacy efforts could have far-reaching effects as we all work toward building brighter futures together.

1. Education and Awareness: You as an advocate have an integral part to play in raising awareness about flaws in criminal justice system. By sharing information, personal stories, or research findings you can educate others of its shortcomings while galvanizing them to take positive steps forward to reform.

2. Grassroots Organizing: Advocacy often begins at a grassroots level, when individuals work collectively to bring about change within their local communities. By holding community meetings and workshops focused on criminal justice reform advocacy, you can engage with others who share your interest while developing strategies,

building alliances and amplifying collective voice - an approach often called grassroots organizing.

3. Policy Advocacy: One effective method for advocating criminal justice reform is engaging policymakers at local, state, and national levels - such as writing letters to elected officials or meeting them face to face - to express concerns or propose specific reforms. By sharing experiences and insights that prioritize rehabilitation, fairness, and equity you can help shape policies that emphasize these aspects of reform.

4. Collaborative Partnerships: Partnership is key when driving real change. By joining forces with organizations, activists, and experts working in criminal justice reform you can combine resources, networks, knowledge sharing to maximize impact and attack issues more holistically. Collaborative efforts provide greater impact than working alone while taking on complex problems from multiple directions simultaneously.

5. Media and Communications: Media is an invaluable asset when it comes to shaping public opinion and informing policymaking decisions. You as an advocate can leverage media outlets by sharing your viewpoint through interviews or writing articles for publication; engaging them can raise public awareness, challenge misconceptions and foster informed discourse around criminal justice reform issues.

6. Mobilize Support: Establishing broad support is integral to creating sustainable change. Mobilizing individu-

als, communities and organizations into an effective advocacy force by organizing rallies, protests and public campaigns on criminal justice reform can bring attention and garner support for specific policies initiatives.

7. Legislative Advocacy: Engaging directly in the legislative process can have a dramatic effect on shaping criminal justice policies. By monitoring proposed bills, attending hearings and providing testimony at these proceedings, you can effectively influence lawmakers to create reforms consistent with principles such as fairness, equity and rehabilitation.

8. Promoting Alternatives to Incarceration: As an advocate, you can champion community-based alternatives to incarceration such as diversion programs, restorative justice practices and expanding treatment and rehabilitation services. By emphasizing successful programs with evidence-based approaches you can help shift the emphasis from punishment towards rehabilitation thereby decreasing recidivism rates.

9. Supporting Impacted Individuals' Voices: Hearing directly from those directly affected by criminal justice system is of utmost importance, so as an advocate you should provide a platform for ex-incarcerated people to share their stories, perspectives, and insights - amplifying these voices helps humanize issues like this one while dispelling stereotypes while advocating for their dignity and rights as individuals involved.

10. Persistence and Long-term Commitment: Real change within the criminal justice system requires persistence and long-term dedication from advocates; advocacy shouldn't be seen as one-time effort but as part of an ongoing journey for reform. By remaining involved and committed, advocates contribute towards this ongoing movement for criminal justice reform.

So, in conclusion, joining the community of advocates for criminal justice reform offers you an opportunity to make real change in people's lives affected by its failings. By raising awareness, engaging in grassroots organizing activities, advocating policy modifications and mobilising support you can contribute towards creating a brighter future where justice, fairness and rehabilitation come first. By joining forces we can challenge status quo issues, dismantle systemic inequities and build an equitable criminal justice system which upholds and benefits everyone in society; your advocacy matters! Together we can bring about lasting change that lasts long-term.

Transitioning out of prison offers an unprecedented chance to effect positive change. We must recognize that individuals leaving prison possess untapped potential that needs unlocking through providing support and resources - we can then unlock those talents to lead fulfilling and productive lives.

Building an inclusive society for individuals transitioning from incarceration requires joint efforts by community members, organizations, policymakers and stakeholders alike. By joining our voices and expertise together we can address the unique issues individuals reentering society face while crafting comprehensive solutions to overcome them.

Rehabilitation should be at the core of our approach to justice. Instead of solely emphasizing punishment, we should emphasize programs and initiatives which support individuals to address underlying causes for their incarceration - education, vocational training, mental health treatment programs and employment opportunities can be key elements in effective rehabilitation, providing individuals with tools they need to rebuild their lives while contributing positively to society.

Accessing resources and opportunities is crucial. Many individuals leaving incarceration face immense barriers when trying to access housing, employment, healthcare and other essential services; therefore addressing them requires comprehensive support - transitional housing programs, job training initiatives and partnerships with employers offering second chances are just some ways in which we can ensure basic needs of individuals are met in order to ensure successful reintegration into society.

Fostering an understanding and accepting culture is paramount in supporting those transitioning from incarceration, an experience often filled with barriers and stigmatism. Therefore, we must fight stereotypes, challenge biases, foster understanding and promote empathy within communities - creating an atmosphere which values second chances while believing in change - providing individuals who may need support when transitioning back into society after having been imprisoned with an environment which supports and embraces them in doing so.

Collective efforts are necessary for lasting changes to be achieved in systemic issues. In order to enact long-lasting transformations, we need to advocate for policy reforms that support fair sentencing, reduce recidivism, and prioritize rehabilitation - something which includes engaging lawmakers, attending community dialogues and raising awareness on criminal justice reform needs. By joining efforts, together we can shape policies and systems which facilitate successful reentry while creating more just societies.

By emphasizing positive change and the importance of collective efforts, we can foster an atmosphere conducive to those transitioning out of prison. Through rehabilitation services, accessing resources and opportunities, advocating system changes, creating understanding among peers, advocating system changes ourselves and making collective actions count towards making a real difference and building communities where redemption and success exist for all.

Last words of advice and motivation.

As someone who has gone through this same transition process myself, let me offer you my support and insight as you embark on their own transition journeys from prison.

Reclaiming Freedom

Although your road ahead might appear challenging at first, let me assure you it will ultimately prove worthwhile in every respect.

No one should define themselves by past mistakes; those mistakes don't determine who we are today or our potential in the future. Each person possesses the power to change, grow and create a brighter future for themselves and those they love.

Remain strong and believe in yourself throughout this challenging journey, remembering to embrace each challenge as an opportunity for growth and evolution. Turn struggles into building blocks towards an improved future!

Surround yourself with positive influences. Seek support from those who genuinely want you to succeed and are willing to offer assistance on the path toward it. Everyone needs someone they can count on when times get rough - when needed most, don't be ashamed to lean on others for assistance!

Utilize all available resources. There are people and organizations out there eager to assist your success; don't be shy about asking for assistance and seeking guidance; whether that means finding employment, accessing education programs or getting counseling, there are resources out there available to you in support of your journey.

Believe in second chances; give yourself the gift of second chances by seizing this opportunity to reconstruct and enhance your life in positive ways. Take this momentous chance to carve a different path, knowing you possess all of the strength within to face any challenges which might present themselves along the way.

Celebrate every step forward as an accomplishment worthy of celebration - no matter how small. When life doesn't go according to plan, don't beat yourself up too harshly for failing to meet expectations; what matters is that you remain moving in an upward trajectory regardless of its speed or pace.

Experiences can serve as powerful sources of motivation. By sharing your story and encouraging change through dialogue and example, you can show others there is hope for a brighter future.

Remember, you aren't on this journey alone - many others have gone down this same road and now stand as living proof of resilience and determination's transformative power. Working together, we can all support one another as individuals while strengthening and amplifying collective voices - increasing impactful voices throughout.

As you embark upon this next chapter of your life, remember to keep your head held high and remain true to yourself. Trust in the potential buried within, knowing you possess enough strength and resilience to overcome any challenges which come your way. Although the journey may be long, remember you are capable of building an amazing future full of hope, joy, and success for you and those around you!

Reclaiming Freedom

Your future is yours to create, so take control and shape it to be exactly how you envision it. Don't get bogged down in the past; life begins afresh now - never forget that! Keep pushing forward; never lose hope that happiness and fulfillment awaits YOU ALL.

Final Words

Ladies and gentleman, Today I bring to you my message of hope, resilience, and unflinching belief in second chances. Each one of you has encountered obstacles on their respective journeys that few could imagine experiencing first-hand; but please know that your past does not dictate your future; rather you possess all of the power within to overcome circumstances to create lives filled with purpose, success and joy!

I want all of you to know that their are great promise in each one of you. By reading this book shows your strength, resolve, and eagerness to change; already taking this first step toward writing your new narrative deserves our greatest admiration and congratulations for taking that initiative!

Remind yourself that it may not be easy - redemption and reintegration require facing numerous external and internal barriers on our journey towards recovery and reconciliation. But remember: our character develops from trials both external and internal; through them all comes resilience, resourcefulness, and new insights which can propel you toward greatness!

Believe in your capacity for change and positive growth; trust that mistakes made do not define who you are; rather they serve as milestones on the road towards personal transformation and self-improvement.

Take the time to identify your strengths and talents. Explore new passions and interests; seek education or skill-building programs which empower you to explore alternative career paths; surround yourself with people who believe in your potential and support you along your journey; remember success is not an endpoint but an ongoing endeavor of personal and professional growth!

While society may place restrictions and judgments upon you, it's vital that you remember your past doesn't define you. With determination and perseverance you are capable of rising above obstacles to prove to the world that you are more than what has gone before - show others the transformative potential inherent within us all!

As you progress forward, keep self-care and compassion top of mind. Make time to heal, forgive yourself and appreciate the amazing human experiences around us all. Surround yourself with positivity, gratitude and mindfulness for a more satisfying journey ahead. Celebrate small victories along the way while learning from setbacks;

Final Words

every day is an opportunity for growth and self-improvement!

Finally, I want you to remember that you're not on this journey alone. There are numerous people and organizations out there dedicated to supporting, guiding and advocating for your success - mentors, community resources or support networks can provide essential assistance and advice when necessary.

As I wrap this letter up, let me assure you that your past does not define who you are today; rather, your resilience and courage make up who you are as an individual - embrace each new chapter with open arms knowing you hold power to rewrite its narrative and build a meaningful and fulfilling future.

Remember it is never too late to dream, achieve, and leave an indelible mark on this world. Your journey may have been difficult at times but has given you strength, wisdom, and perseverance necessary for overcoming any challenge along your journey. Your unique contributions await recognition by everyone around you - so never stop dreaming and making positive steps forward in life!

Believe in yourself and seize every opportunity that awaits. Your light doesn't come from what has come before but from who you are now; its source lies within. Don't limit yourself by what's happened before; see all that potential within yourself that awaits to shine outward!

Sources

Chapter Four

1. High Prevalence of Mental Health Disorders:

- According to a study published in the American Journal of Public Health, individuals leaving incarceration have a higher prevalence of mental health disorders compared to the general population (Binswanger et al., 2010).

- The Substance Abuse and Mental Health Services Administration (SAMHSA) reported that approximately 56% of state prisoners, 45% of federal prisoners, and 64% of jail inmates have a mental health problem (James & Glaze, 2006).

2. Co-Occurrence of Substance Abuse and Mental Health Issues:

Sources

- Many individuals transitioning from incarceration struggle with co-occurring mental health and substance use disorders.

- The National Institute on Drug Abuse (NIDA) states that substance abuse and mental health issues often intersect, with substance use serving as a form of self-medication for underlying mental health conditions (NIDA, 2018).

3. Barriers to Accessing Mental Health Care:

- Formerly incarcerated individuals face significant barriers in accessing mental health services and support.

- A report by the Council of State Governments Justice Center found that individuals leaving incarceration often experience limited access to healthcare, lack of insurance coverage, and insufficient community resources (CSG Justice Center, 2017).

4. Impact of Incarceration on Mental Health:

- The experience of incarceration itself can exacerbate or contribute to mental health issues.

- Research published in JAMA Psychiatry suggests that the trauma, stress, and stigmatization associated with incarceration can lead to or worsen mental health problems (Wang et al., 2018).

5. Importance of Comprehensive Reentry Programs:

Sources

- Comprehensive reentry programs that address mental health needs are crucial for successful community reintegration.

- The RAND Corporation conducted a study highlighting the effectiveness of comprehensive programs that provide mental health services, substance abuse treatment, and other support in reducing recidivism and improving mental health outcomes (Davis et al., 2013).

Addressing the mental health needs of individuals transitioning from incarceration requires a multi-faceted approach that includes increased access to mental health care, targeted interventions, and comprehensive reentry support. By recognizing the prevalence of mental health challenges in this population and implementing evidence-based strategies, we can work towards better outcomes and support successful community reintegration.

Sources:

- Binswanger, I. A., et al. (2010). Medical Conditions, Medications, and

Medical Emergencies in Jail: A Review. American Journal of Public Health, 100(12), 2382–2391.

- Council of State Governments Justice Center. (2017). Stepping Up: A

National Initiative to Reduce the Number of People with Mental Illnesses in Jails.

Sources

- Davis, L. M., et al. (2013). How Effective Is Correctional Education, and

Where Do We Go from Here? The Results of a Comprehensive Evaluation. RAND Corporation.

- James, D. J., & Glaze, L. E. (2006). Mental Health Problems of Prison and

Jail Inmates. Bureau of Justice Statistics.

- National Institute on Drug Abuse. (2018). Comorbidity: Substance Use

Disorders and Other Mental Illnesses.

Social support plays a crucial role in the successful reentry process for individuals transitioning from incarceration to society. It provides emotional, practical, and relational assistance that can help mitigate challenges and promote positive outcomes. Here are some key points on the significance of social support during reentry, supported by relevant sources:

1. Emotional Support:

- Emotional support from family, friends, mentors, or support groups can help individuals cope with the emotional stress and isolation often experienced during reentry.

- According to a study published in the Journal of Offender Rehabilitation, emotional support positively influences mental well-being and reduces recidivism rates among formerly incarcerated individuals (Maruna & LeBel, 2019).

2. Practical Support:

- Practical support, such as assistance with housing, employment, transportation, and accessing healthcare, can help individuals address immediate needs and create stability in their lives.

- The Council of State Governments Justice Center emphasizes the importance of practical support in reentry programs, highlighting its role in reducing recidivism rates and supporting successful community reintegration (CSG Justice Center, 2018).

3. Peer Support:

- Peer support programs, where individuals with lived experiences of incarceration provide guidance and encouragement, have shown to be effective in promoting positive change during reentry.

- The National Institute of Justice recognizes the value of peer support in addressing the unique challenges faced by formerly incarcerated individuals, including social isolation and reintegration difficulties (NIJ, 2018).

4. Community Networks:

- Building connections with supportive community networks, such as faith-based organizations, community centers, and local resources, can provide individuals with a sense of belonging and a network of people invested in their success.

- The RAND Corporation's report on reentry programs highlights the importance of community engagement and collaboration to foster social support and facilitate successful reentry (Davis et al., 2013).

5. Mentoring and Role Models:

- Mentoring programs that pair individuals with mentors who have successfully navigated reentry can provide guidance, support, and inspiration for personal growth and positive change.

- A study published in the Journal of Community Psychology found that mentoring relationships positively impact post-release outcomes, including employment, housing stability, and overall well-being (Geller et al., 2019).

Chapter Five

- Council of State Governments Justice Center. (2018). The Integrated

Reentry and Employment Strategies Implementation Study: Findings from the Evaluation of Nine Sites.

- Davis, L. M., et al. (2013). How Effective Is Correctional Education, and

Sources

Where Do We Go from Here? The Results of a Comprehensive Evaluation. RAND Corporation.

- Geller, A., et al. (2019). The Effects of Mentoring on Post-Release Outcomes for Individuals Returning to Communities After Incarceration: A Randomized Experiment. Journal of Community Psychology, 47(4), 852-866.

- Maruna, S., & LeBel, T. P. (2019). Through Desistance and Back Again? A Review of the Literature on the Role of Support in Offender Desistance and Recidivism. Journal of Offender Rehabilitation, 58(5), 436-462.

- National Institute of Justice. (2018). The Role of Peer Support in Reentry. Office of Justice Programs.

Sources:

- Binswanger, I. A., et al. (2010). Medical Conditions, Medications, and Medical Emergencies in Jail: A Review. American Journal of Public Health, 100(12), 2382–2391.

- Council of State Governments Justice Center. (2017). Stepping Up: A National Initiative to Reduce the Number of People with Mental Illnesses in Jails.

- Davis, L. M., et al. (2013). How Effective Is Correctional Education, and

Where Do We Go from Here? The Results of a Comprehensive Evaluation. RAND Corporation.

- James, D. J., & Glaze, L. E. (2006). Mental Health Problems of Prison and

Jail Inmates. Bureau of Justice Statistics.

- National Institute on Drug Abuse. (2018). Comorbidity: Substance Use

Disorders and Other Mental Illnesses.

Chapter Seven

Sources:

1. Substance Abuse and Mental Health Services Administration (SAMHSA). (n.d.). Access to Mental Health Services: Barriers and Interventions. Retrieved from https://www.samhsa.gov/sites/default/files/access-mental-health-services.pdf

2. World Health Organization (WHO). (2021). Mental health: Strengthening our response. Retrieved from https://www.who.int/news-room/fact-sheets/detail/mental-health-strengthening-our-response

Sources

3. National Institute of Mental Health (NIMH). (2020). Rural Mental Health. Retrieved from https://www.nimh.nih.gov/health/topics/rural-mental-health

4. Office of Minority Health (OMH). (2020). Improving Cultural Competency for Behavioral Health Professionals. Retrieved from https://www.minorityhealth.hhs.gov/omh/browse.aspx?lvl=3&lvlid=64

Notes

Notes

www.ingramcontent.com/pod-product-compliance
Lightning Source LLC
Chambersburg PA
CBHW070255230526
45470CB00002B/598